From Authority to Friendship

For those of us with adult children, navigating the transition from childhood to adulthood rarely comes with clear instructions. Thankfully, Tim Goeman has done the hard work of thinking carefully and biblically through what this season ought to look like—and how parents should walk through it faithfully. I am grateful for Goeman's clear commitment to biblical principles and his willingness to help parents push through mixed emotions in order to act in ways that honor God and genuinely serve their adult children as wise, gracious friends. If you are approaching this stage of life, get this book and prayerfully work through it. If you know someone already there, give them a copy and pray God will use it for its intended good.

Dr. Mike Fabarez
Pastor of Compass Bible Church, Aliso Viejo, California
Author of *Raising Men, Not Boys* (Moody Publishers, 2017)

The relationship between parents and their adult children can be complicated. All parties need wisdom. This book provides a wealth of practical biblically based advice for how parents can cultivate a relationship of mutual respect with their adult children.

Dr. Jim Newheiser
Professor of Christian Counseling and Pastoral Theology
Director of the Christian Counseling Program
Reformed Theological Seminary, Charlotte

Tim Goeman's *From Authority to Friendship: Navigating New Seasons with Adult Children* is a delightful read for three reasons. First, as a dad of adult children, it applied to me immediately. Second, as a pastor, I was so pleased to receive this well-needed and practical resource. Third, as a theologian, I was comforted to observe the whole book anchored firmly in Scripture. Crafted in a compact and easy-to-read style, this is precisely what Christian parents of adult children need. This is a *must-read* without a doubt.

Dr. Steve Swartz
Senior Pastor of Grace Bible Church of Bakersfield
Author of *Abuse, Abandonment, and Divorce*, *Strength in the River*, and *Profile of a Godly Wife*

From Authority
to Friendship

Navigating New Seasons
with Adult Children

Tim Goeman

SOJOURNER
PRESS

Cover design by Sojourner Press

For bulk, special sales, or ministry purchases, please contact us at sales@sojournerpress.org.

From Authority to Friendship:
Navigating New Seasons with Adult Children
Copyright © 2026 by Tim Goeman
Published by Sojourner Press
PO Box 37441
Raleigh, NC, 27626
sojournerpress.org

Trade paperback ISBN: 978-1-960255-19-8
ePub ISBN: 978-1-960255-20-4
Audiobook ISBN: 978-1-960255-21-1

Printed in the United States of America

DEDICATION

*This book is dedicated to my wife,
Julie, the love of my life.*

I lean toward being a pretty black-and-white guy,
often forgetting that Christian parenting and church life
are rarely as simple as I would like them to be.
She regularly reminds me that our relationships
must always be seasoned with the appropriate
measures of love and compassion.
She has truly been a helper fit for me,
as God intended.

Contents

Foreword

In a world of fractured families and self-focused pursuits, it's sadly common to see strained relationships between parents and their adult children. It doesn't have to be that way. God designed family life to continue after the kids leave home, and this season can become one of His sweetest gifts to maturing parents.

As both a son and a churchman, I've seen this up close. My father, Tim Goeman, has long been one of the voices I trust most. When he told me he was writing about the relationship between parents and their adult children, I knew it would serve the church well. Parenting is already a tender area; the transition from authority to friendship is where many stumble—sometimes late, sometimes never. By God's grace, my brothers and I count our dad among our closest friends. In *From Authority to Friendship: Navigating New Seasons with Adult Children*, he offers biblically rich, hard-won wisdom so more families can say the same.

I should note that, growing up, my brothers and I occasionally drove my parents crazy. We often drove my mom up the wall with our juvenile tendencies. However, she always had the trump card when she would say, "We'll deal with this when your father gets home." And my father certainly dealt with it, bringing appropriate authority and consequence to us wayward boys. But the relationship didn't stay in the realm of authoritative interactions. As we matured, our parents intentionally shifted from an authoritative position to that of wise counselors. I've watched (and experienced as a son) that transition, practiced with patience and humility, bear good fruit for decades.

This book lays the theological foundation for that shift and then wades into the practical questions parents actually face: wedding expectations, grandparenting dynamics, avoiding favoritism, and navigating technology. A concise FAQ is also included, addressing the sticky scenarios everyone thinks about but few want to name out loud.

Christians have long recognized that parenting is one of our most important callings. Too often zeal isn't matched with biblical wisdom and practice. My prayer is that these pages will supply both, so that moms and dads can bless their adult children and point them to Christ.

I am so thankful for this book. It is biblical, wise, and gives insight into family relationships that can last a lifetime.

Peter Goeman
Associate Professor of OT and Biblical Languages
Shepherds Theological Seminary
Cary, North Carolina — January 2026

Introduction

Parenting is hard work. Christian parenting is even more difficult as Christians attempt to incorporate biblical principles into their parenting methods—or more correctly, biblical principles direct the parents' entire approach to parenting. Wise Christian parents often seek out training resources through their local church as they embark on the daunting task of raising children in a way that is pleasing to the Lord.

After a couple of decades of "parenting in the trenches" as their children grow from infants to young adults, many parents feel a sense of relief that "it's finally over." However, nothing could be further from the truth. The reality is that the Christian life is largely about relationships. Relationships between parents and their children change as children grow up. Parents must also change and view their relationships with their adult children biblically.

It is true enough that the years of training young children and counseling adolescents has ended, but now there are some young adults in your life that were not there previously. How should parents relate to these young adults that are now on the scene? Has anyone helped parents prepare for these years? Are the interactions between parents and their adult kids the same as they have been in the past? Does this topic even need any attention, or will it all "just work out?"

As a church elder and counselor, I can assure you that this is a topic that cannot be left to chance, assuming that everything "will just work out okay." I can make this assertion with great confidence because the Bible has a lot to say about how parents need to relate to their adult children. I have also observed the devastating results in relationships where Christian parents were unaware of the scriptural directives on these issues or chose to ignore them because "they knew better."

Christian parents, the years when your children are adults can be some of the sweetest of your life, but only if you understand these new relationships as God intended them to function. To that end I have compiled this book. We must understand that these evolving relationships are part of what God has intended to be "very good."

Chapter 1

The Goal of Parenting

All parents want their children to succeed in life. But the definition of success varies from parent to parent. Success for some might mean a lucrative salary and financial independence. For others, success might hinge on having a position of power, such as leading a large company or wielding significant political influence. Success for others might be a bit more down-to-earth—graduating from college, getting a good job, being able to afford a nice house, or making a contribution to society. While Christian parents are included among those who want their children to succeed, the Bible defines success much differently than what the world might typically express. For Christians, I'll offer that the following definition more closely aligns with what the Scriptures have to say about success: *The goal of Christian parenting is to raise up adults who know the God of the Bible and are prepared to interact with their culture from a biblical worldview while being fully independent and functional.* In essence, starting at the child's birth, Christian parents are strategically working to put themselves out of a job. Other Christian counselors have stated it this way: "childhood was designed to be a temporary season of training—a time to equip children to live as wise, independent adults."[1] Similarly, MacArthur states:

---

1 Jim Newheiser and Elyse Fitzpatrick, *You Never Stop Being a Parent: Thriving in Relationship with Your Adult Children* (Phillipsburg, NJ: P & R Publishing, 2010), 17.

> "The bulk of every parent's responsibility is training children to be discerning. We continually do it, even when our kids become teenagers. We help them think through issues, understand what is wise and unwise, and prompt them to make the right choices. We help them discern. In fact, the goal of parenting is to raise a discerning child. It doesn't happen automatically, and it doesn't occur without diligent, lifelong instruction."[2]

In short, parents are called to prepare their children for life!

Knowing God

Let's examine the four components of my definition, starting with the most important piece. We must give our maximum effort in helping our children know the God of the Bible. I fully understand that God is totally sovereign in salvation, but parents must view themselves as the primary tool through which God can accomplish the salvation of their children. This can never be simply left to chance, to Sunday school teachers or to a pastor.

"Parents are called to prepare their children for life!"

Parents are on the front line in the battle for the souls of their children. Christian parents should have scheduled, structured time for teaching their children

---

2 John MacArthur, *Fool's Gold? Discerning Truth in an Age of Error* (Wheaton, IL: Crossway, 2005), 206.

the Bible, but also be very deliberate in training their children in righteousness (2 Tim. 3:16). This means explaining all instruction and correction within the context of God's love and what He requires of people according to his Word, always making it age-appropriate. For a full discussion of the necessity of "training in righteousness," see *Teach Them Diligently*.[3] Further, parents must understand that they represent God to their children until they attain an age where they can grasp biblical concepts and develop their own relationships with their God and Savior. For example, at a very young age, my wife and I were diligent in teaching our children table manners during all meal times. When they were young, they only understood that certain behaviors were unacceptable and certain other behaviors were required. As they became older they understood that these rules were putting into action the biblical notion of thinking of others as more important that yourself. Wallace illustrates this concept when she explains that teaching our kids to fear God makes our discipline less about us and more about their relationship to God.[4] Eventually, we parents should work ourselves out of the job as middleman between God and our children.

---

3 Lou Priolo, *Teach Them Diligently: How to Use the Scriptures in Child Training* (Woodruff, SC: Timeless Texts, 2000).

4 Sara Wallace, *For the Love of Discipline: When the Gospel Meets Tantrums and Timeouts* (Phillipsburg, NJ: P&R Publishing, 2018), 44-46, 149.

A Biblical Worldview

We should also desire that our children learn to interact effectively with our culture from a biblical worldview. Most Christian parents, at some point during their parenting years, secretly (or not so secretly) wish they could whisk their children away to some remote environment where they could be protected forever from this evil age. Such a concept is foreign to Scripture. Believers are saved to be salt and light (Matt. 5:13-16) and to accomplish the good things that God has prepared for them to do. Further, although we recognize that we live in "this present evil age," the gospel never promises to remove us from the world, but rather to empower us to overcome the evil age in which we live (Gal. 1:4; John 17:15; Rom. 12:2).

What do I mean by "worldview?" Broadly, a worldview is a collection of attitudes, values, and expectations about the world around us which inform our every thought and action. Everyone has a worldview. It is how we see and process everything around us. More specifically, a biblical worldview is an all-encompassing view of the world based on God's revealed truth, which directs our life in this world.

A biblical worldview shapes our beliefs about God, creation, humanity, what is morally right, man's purpose, suffering, work, eternity, government, money, the future, and any other topic or issue you can think of. A biblical worldview shapes how we think, how we act, and who we really are in every area of our lives. A Christian with a well-developed biblical worldview will interact with the culture in a way that is entirely biblical and, therefore, entirely pleasing to God.

Of course, in reality, no Christian interacts perfectly with the world. But that is because our knowledge and application of the Bible and its principles are deficient at some level. That is why we all continue to learn and grow—the Holy Spirit's sanctifying work in us will continue throughout our lives. This part of our definition simply means that you set your children on the right course of having a biblical worldview, which will continue to be refined over the course of their lives as they take in and understand more Scripture. Furthermore, consider the reality that the next generation (your children) must accurately represent God and the principles of His Word to their contemporaries because our aging generation will soon fade out of the picture of influence.

Independence

We should want our children to grow up to be independent. By this I mean not dependent on their parents but dependent on God and having vital interdependent relationships within their local church. Practically, this means we steer our children toward being able to support themselves financially as a normal course of their lives. Children must be trained to understand biblical stewardship. They must understand how finances work from a biblical perspective. Food, housing, transportation, debt, medical care, giving and recreation are all financial realities that every functional, mature adult must be able to grasp and manage well. The credibility of their Christian life will depend, in part, on "managing their household well" (1 Tim. 3:4; Titus 1:7-8). For Christian parents who may have some resistance to this concept, consider another reality: statistically, you will die before your children. Long before this happens, wise parents will ensure their children are fully independent of them.

I have an eight-year-old grandson who has had diabetes since the age of three. At age three he was not able to administer his own life-sustaining insulin. But, as an eight-year-old, his parents are wisely moving him toward being able to manage his medical needs independently. At his current stage, he is obviously not fully independent regarding his medical needs, but he is being trained to administer his own insulin and monitor his own blood sugar level. He is on track to be independent in this realm within a few years. If children do not learn how to live life independently from their parents, who will they learn it from?

Functional

The last piece of the definition I have offered is striving to raise children who are functional. Functionality is multifaceted. The most important facet of this functionality revolves around the local church. Do your children know how they are gifted, and are they using those gifts to edify the local church body for the common good (1 Cor. 12:7)? Failure to function in this arena will leave a person unfulfilled and will leave a hole in the local church. It is essential.

When my middle son was 10 years old, I volunteered to coach his summer baseball team. Each team had 12 or 13 players, so if everyone showed up for the games, we could easily field the nine players required. Sometimes only seven or eight players showed up for our games. We still played the games but were obviously short-handed and the team could not perform as well as they did when we had nine or more players. Not only did the team suffer, but the players who missed games regularly did not develop as they should have in their playing ability. The analogy here is that the church suffers when members are absent, but the believer also suffers because they are not maturing as they otherwise might if they were ministering regularly in the local church.

Additionally, this functionality includes a relationship with society. Christians are called to be *in the world* but not of the world (John 17:14-18). Our young adults must become involved in the world around them in meaningful ways. Assuming they can work, they should be working (motherhood can be full-time work). They should pay their taxes. They should vote. As they have interest and ability, they should be involved in their community—improving it for the common good, in whatever form that may take. This functionality is the antithesis of being sequestered away with no contact or interest in the society around you.[5] Sending your child off to join a monastery is not a biblical concept! Clearly, such an approach cannot mesh with the command to "go into all the world" (Mark 16:15).

Christian parents must keep the goal of parenting in mind, even as they are in the trenches. I realize there are days when kids take so much energy that parents can hardly catch their breath, let alone keep their goal

---

5 John MacArthur, *Successful Christian Parenting: Raising Your Child with Care, Compassion, and Common Sense* (Nashville, TN: Word Publishing, 1998), 35-40.

in mind. Nevertheless, as that baby grows into a toddler and then a young child headed toward adolescence, there will be opportunities to parent toward the end goal. Christian parents must not miss those opportunities.[6]

---

6 Mike Fabarez, *Raising Men, Not Boys* (Chicago, IL: Moody Publishers, 2017), 21-30, 105-121, 188-189.

Chapter 2
Biblical Authority

As Christian parents, Amy and Bruce were very close to their daughter, Diana. They spoke on the phone almost daily through Diana's four years of college. Amy had freely given her advice about a number of young men Diana had dated during the college years and was thrilled (and a bit relieved) when Diana told her about a new Christian suitor, William, who would be graduating at the same time as Diana, and was the top mechanical engineer in his class. Shortly after graduation, Diana and William were married, and both were employed near Bruce and Amy's home. It seemed to Amy and Bruce like a perfect world. Then one day, Amy got a call from Diana informing her that William had taken a big promotion with his company and would be heading the company division in Saudi Arabia! Diana was very excited and told her mother they would be moving next month.

After the initial shock of the news wore off, Amy began her campaign to change the course of future history. She told Diana and William that she would not allow them to move. This action would be unbiblical since God designed family units to be close physically and spiritually. She also made it clear that making this move would directly violate her and Bruce's authority as their parents. Did Bruce and Amy have authority in the lives of William and Diana?

The Difference between Biblical Authority and Worldly Authority

Much of the misunderstanding regarding difficult relationships between Christian parents and their children is rooted in unbiblical concepts of authority. Biblical authority is very different than the authority seen and practiced in our sin-marred world. Essentially, biblical authority is lovingly directed toward achieving compliance with a biblical command or principle because that is what God wants from us. Interestingly, biblical authority always organizes, builds, encourages, and it always loves.[1] Think of biblical authority as that which has been authorized by God.[2]

In contrast to biblical authority, worldly authority demands, "Do it my way, or else." Is it any wonder that we live in a world where it seems everyone is chafing against authority? This is largely due to the abuse of power by those in positions of authority who are using it for their own selfish ends. Parents aren't the only ones who can abuse power—coaches, politicians, business leaders, and even law enforcement officers can, too.

Not surprisingly, people generally have a sinful inclination to use their positions of authority for their own

---

1 Jonathan Leeman, "Complementarianism: A Moment of Reckoning (Part 3)," *9Marks*, December 11, 2019, https://www.9marks.org/article/complementarianism-a-moment-of-reckoning-part-3/.

2 Jonathan Leeman, "Authority: God's Good and Dangerous Gift," *9Marks*, September 26, 2016, https://www.9marks.org/article/authority-gods-good-and-dangerous-gift/.

benefit.[3] And for unbelievers, they really have no reason to think or act differently (Rom. 8:7-8). Christians, however, have the capacity to think differently and act righteously because of the indwelling Holy Spirit. Christian parents must never fall into the error of wielding worldly authority over their children. Unfortunately, in our example, Bruce and Amy were clinging desperately to what they knew of worldly authority and were leaving a trail of destruction in its wake.

> "Christian parents must never fall into the error of wielding worldly authority over their children."

Think for a moment how this practically unfolds during the life of a child. As a baby, parents have complete authority over their little bundle of joy simply because this baby cannot do anything for himself. As toddlers, the children start thinking for themselves and are capable of physical accomplishments. Their understanding is still immature, so parents are still deeply involved in instruction and training (use of authority) according to scriptural standards. As children become preteens and then teens, their capacity to understand what God wants for their lives should become more deeply ingrained in their hearts, so ideally, there is a seamless transition from functioning under the parent's authority to living obediently for God. This progression from living under authority to having more responsibility is a natural outworking of God's design for the family.

---

3 Ibid.

What Biblical Authority is Not

Before leaving the topic of biblical authority, it may be helpful to provide several examples of what biblical authority is not. The pastor who declares to his congregation that "you must follow me without question" is not exercising biblical authority. In fact, he has no authority beyond preaching the Word accurately, and then the Word proclaimed carries God's authority.[4] Unfortunately, the religious landscape is strewn with the wreckage of leaders who abused their authority, developed a cult-like following and then inevitably self-destructed, ruining many lives as they did so. With this history, it is understandable why so many people view all religion with suspicion.

Likewise, the father who makes demands of his children without clear links to specific Scripture is not exercising biblical authority. Vaguely lumping all parental commands under "children obey your parents" is a failure to fulfill all that God intends for parents. My point is simply that a position, whether pastor or parent, does not give *carte blanche* authority for issuing commands. Those in these positions must only use the authority that God has *authorized*, and then they must wield that authority very carefully.

---

4 See, for example, John MacArthur on what authority a pastor has over his congregation (https://www.youtube.com/watch?v=X65vspiZLLA). See also, Todd Friel's comments on MacArthur's statement (https://www.youtube.com/watch?v=EWq9rJzTdzY).

Using the Scriptures as Authorized

I have had the privilege of being an elder in our local church for over 20 years and frequently counsel people who are struggling with serious life issues. Regardless of the specific issue, one principle that must be stressed during biblical counseling is that the counselor is not authorized to make decisions for the counselee. Decisions can only be made by the counselee as the Holy Spirit through the Scriptures moves the heart. As a counselor, I can tell them what the Scriptures say about the issue they are facing, and then with this information, they will be equipped to take the action that will honor God. However, it would be wrong and potentially harmful for me to impose more on people than the all-sufficient Scriptures convey.[5]

Understanding biblical authority prepares parents and children for healthy relationships as children move into their adult years.[6] Without this understanding, no amount of time, debate, or guilt will ever produce what God intended in these relationships.

If Bruce and Amy had understood biblical authority, they could have come alongside their young adults and encouraged them during this time of transition. They may have been a big help with many of the details of the move and paved the way for decades of sweet friendship

---

5 Newheiser and Fitzpatrick, *You Never Stop Being a Parent*, 23-27, 38-39.

6 Janet Aucoin and Jocelyn Wallace, "Biblical Authority," *Joyful Journey Podcast*, April 19, 2024, https://www.faithlafayette. org/resources/podcast/biblical-authority.

with their kids. Instead, they created hardship and may have fractured future relationships beyond repair.

Chapter 3

Children, Obey Your Parents

Does a child ever cease being under the authority of their parents? If so, when and how does this occur? Far too many Christian parents are living under the illusion that as long as they are alive, their children must obey them in all things without question, regardless of the age of the children. Such folly is rooted in a misunderstanding and misapplication of biblical authority and the God-designed changes that must occur in the parent-child relationship.

Ephesians 6:1 tells us, "Children, obey your parents in the Lord, for this is right." Paul gives a similar instruction in Colossians 3:20: "Children, obey your parents in everything, for this pleases the Lord." These short verses lay out the essential, God-designed, and God-approved method for raising young children and relating to older children as they mature. These verses provide an excellent launching point for thinking in detail about God's prescription for parenting.

Parents in Authority

A necessary starting point for this discussion is a biblical understanding of authority (see Chapter 2). Parents are clearly in a position of authority over their young children. Even this simple concept is sometimes misunderstood. Parents, you are not your children's friend. You have the unique and God-assigned role of being their parent. When they are young, your children do not need an adult friend; they need you to fulfill your God-given role as parent. No one else can step into that role for you.

Recall that biblical authority is the God-given moral right to make choices.[1] Your young children are incapable of making correct moral choices, so parents, as God's agents, will do that for them. This includes everything from scheduling nap times, planning what to eat, and mandating the children share toys. In all cases, the children are learning about a functional structure that is right.

> "Biblical authority is the position of providing and protecting."

Additionally, authority loves, gives, encourages, builds, and creates an environment for flourishing.[2] Jesus provided us with the perfect example of biblical authority. He always spoke truth, but was kind and gentle. He offered correction but never lost control. Recall also that biblical authority never "lords it over" others (1 Pet. 5:3). On the contrary, biblical authority is the position of providing and protecting. The greatest advantage always goes to the one under biblical authority rather than the one in authority.[3]

---

1 Leeman, "Authority: God's Good and Dangerous Gift," https://www.9marks.org/article/authority-gods-good-and-dangerous-gift/.

2 Ibid.

3 Leeman, "Complementarianism: A Moment of Reckoning (Part 3)," https://www.9marks.org/article/complementarianism-a-moment-of-reckoning-part-3/.

Some parents go wrong by adopting the world's view of authority. They think in terms of command and control and view their family as a small army where they are the supreme commander. To be sure, parents can achieve external obedience from their children using this approach, but they will never capture their children's hearts. Parents must understand that they are God's agents during their parenting years. Parents represent God to their young children because their children are incapable of understanding God on their own. "Johnny, you need to eat your peas because that's one of the good foods God has given us, and eating them will keep you strong and healthy." Granted, not every one of the hundreds of instructions from parents to their young children will include a direct reference to God, but not a day should go by where God is not a prominent person in the picture. MacArthur states:

> "I think this is very important in the rearing
> of children. You have not satisfied the
> responsibilities of parenthood when you've
> made your child to submit to you. When
> you put so much fear in your child that
> your child is afraid to violate you, that is
> not the end of parenting. You have parented
> your child appropriately when your child
> lives with the fear of God, not you. You're
> an intermediary with the responsibility of
> teaching your child to fear God. I don't want
> my children to just grow up and fear me,

because what are they going to do when I'm not there?"[4]

Far too many parents wonder what went wrong when their child reaches adulthood and then abandons the church and starts living like the world. Typically, such cases involve a child who submitted to their parents out of fear or to avoid conflict, but they never had a heart for God.

Changing Authority

The application of authority changes as a child grows and matures. During the early childhood years, let's say up to about age five, parents have singular authority and they may use biblical chastisement to enforce their commands (Prov. 13:24; 22:15; 29:11). Beyond age five, the rod should rarely be used because this child is now becoming capable of learning about and knowing the God of Scripture, and the parents' role is transitioning from singular authority to a role that points children to the authority of Scripture and the counsel of the wise parents. By the time the young person is in their teens, ideally they have a relationship with God, they understand much of the Scriptures and the kinds of moral choices God requires. At that point, parents have entirely transitioned their authority over to the role of occasional biblical counsel because now Scripture governs the parents'

---

4 John MacArthur, "The Characteristics of True Repentance," *Grace to You*, October 21, 2007, accessed May 9, 2025, https://www.gty.org/library/sermons-library/80-188/the-characteristics-of-true-repentance.

decisions and the decisions of their teens, so there is no difference (in theory). Where differences exist, everyone recognizes these as matters of preference so there are no "hills to die on." Parents must always be loving their children toward God's righteousness.

Of course, this greatly oversimplifies the reality of parenting. There may well be some intense discussions between teenagers and their parents. Sometimes Christian teenagers go through prolonged periods of outright rebellion. Some Christian parents

> **"Parents must always be loving their children toward God's righteousness."**

will admit that the years of parenting their teen were the most difficult of all their years of parenting. At an academic level, the base problem in such cases was a fractured relationship between the teen and God. At times, unbiblical parenting can be added to the mix. However, it is helpful to keep the ideal framework in mind. It is always hard for parents to let go, but wise parents are truly trying to work themselves out of a job, so don't resist the steps that get you there. Sometimes the greatest lessons learned are through our children's poor choices and failures.

Who are Children?

Let's take a moment to consider what we mean by "children" in this discussion—who are they, and how does their level of maturity shape a parent's role? The term used refers to young ones. They are still relying on their parents to meet the basic necessities of life. They are dependent on their parents for the necessities of life because they could not survive on their own. Technically, this can include children of all ages who are living under their parents' roof, but parents will not be treating their 16-year-old the same as their six-year-old.

As previously described, parents are standing in the gap between God and their children while they are too young to have a full and mature relationship with God themselves. Parents are God's stewards. As the child matures, there is no longer the need for a parent standing between them and their God.

Let's talk about age. Up to age 8-10 requires full obedience because parents are representing God and what He requires. During ages 11-15 young people are developing their own moral and spiritual life (it is no longer "because mom and dad said so," but because this is pleasing to God). Ages 16-18 is final preparation time for flying solo (parents are coaching from the sidelines, offering godly counsel when needed). When they are 18, they are adults. They should be ready to leave this "obedience to parents" mode entirely and be living in "obedience to God" mode, but as stated earlier, there should be very little difference. Biblical counselor, Lou Priolo, writes, "Ideally, long before your child leaves home he will be more dependent on his heavenly Father's leading, than he is on yours."[5] Consider my age categories as guidelines. There can be a lot of variability between individual children and families, but there is no valid reason why an 18-year-old in our western world should not be considered an adult.

---

5 Priolo, *Teach Them Diligently*, 53.

As an example of the transition described above, one of my sons reminds me of my counsel to him when he was 18 years old, although I don't remember it quite this way. He was home from college for the summer and wanted to go out for the evening with his friends and asked if it would be okay if he went and was home by midnight. I had no reason in the world to suspect any nefarious activity by him or the friends he hung out with. Apparently, according to my son, I approved his plan by saying that he was now 18 years old and could go to jail for the decisions he made! My son tells me that this was a transformative time in his own life where he realized that we as his parents had handed the reigns over to him to be responsible for his decisions. While my tact may have required some improvement, the facts of my statement were correct. Our society and our judicial system recognize all 18-year-olds as adults. All parents should do the same, regardless of their place of residence. To treat your 18-year-old as anything other than an adult is to shield them from reality and do them a great disservice.

Let's be very transparent here and admit that this is a very difficult phase of parenting. Your young adult sees the world in front of them for the taking without recognizing many of the inherent dangers and difficulties that you know exist. This is especially difficult when you know a decision is not the best and could spell hardships ahead, if not outright disaster. Nonetheless, learning from mistakes is a requirement of maturing.

A Unique Person

A few final thoughts about relating to your young adult. Recognize that your child was made in God's image (Gen. 1:27) and is very unique in their personality, aptitudes, communication style, and individuality. Parents should recognize this individuality by allowing their young adult to select their own vocation, college, spouse, and any other choices that must be made. Hopefully, your relationship will be such that they will welcome and value your input, but in the end, the decision is theirs. These young adults should never be pressured to attend a specific college, join the family business, or enter a profession because there exists a succession of family members who have done this previously. As the parent of an 18 to 24-year-old, if you offer them some assistance, such as help paying for college or loaning them money for a down payment on a house, this does not change their status as an adult, nor does it give the parent any "extra" authority in their lives. I remember hearing about some parents who "gifted" their adult children some plane tickets to manipulate them into coming to see them for Christmas, even though the couple had already made other plans for that holiday season. To use parental "assistance" to leverage behavior is simply sinful manipulation on the part of the parent.

My youngest son's quest for the right college provides a positive example of how this might work. Prior to finishing high school, our son decided to pursue a computer science major in college. He narrowed his college choices to the University of North Dakota in Fargo and The Master's College (now University) in Southern

California. He chose The Master's College, at least in part, thanks to our well-timed March visit to Southern California—which felt like paradise after surviving a Midwest winter. The Master's College was more expensive and much further from home. At the time, we were unsure how we would be able to finance this private college, and he had a health condition that needed regular monitoring, but we supported his decision. In the end, the Lord provided the needed funds, and we all matured in entrusting serious health concerns to the Creator. Looking back, it was one of the best decisions he ever made!

Obedience

Exactly what does the obedience of Ephesians 6:1 and Colossians 3:20 look like? One of the best examples of obedience in Scripture is the account of Samuel, Saul, and Amalek in 1 Samuel 15. Saul did things his own way, and God was not pleased with him. From this account, we can clearly learn what God expects in the way of obedience, and it is a high standard. True obedience is complete and immediate. It is not interlaced with human manipulations and ideas. Partial obedience is disobedience. Delayed obedience is disobedience. Modified obedience is disobedience.

Why is the standard for obedience so high? Parents, you are God's representative to your children. From you, they will learn to obey God or learn some variation of quasi-obedience that is, in reality, disobedience. Remember Samuel's words to Saul: "To obey is better than sacrifice" (1 Sam. 15:22).

All children need training in obedience simply because all are born in a state of total depravity. This means their natural predisposition is toward sin and away from God. John Ellington, a professor of criminal law at the University of Minnesota, said this to the United States Congress in 1960:

> "It must be remembered that no infant is born a finished product. On the contrary, every baby starts life as a little savage. He is equipped among other things with organs and muscles over which he has no control, with an urge for self-preservation, with aggressive drives, and emotions like anger, fear, and love over which likewise he has practically no control. He is completely selfish and self-centered. He wants what he wants when he wants it—his bottle, his mother's attention, his playmate's toy, his uncle's watch. Deny those wants and he seethes with rage and aggression which could be murderous were he not so helpless. He is dirty, he has no manners, no shame, no respect for persons or property, no conscience, no morals, no knowledge, no skills.
>
> What I am saying, of course, is that all children, not just certain children, are born delinquent. If permitted to continue in the self-centered world of his infancy, giving free rein to his impulsive actions to satisfy his wants, every child would grow up a criminal—a thief, a killer, a rapist."[6]

---

6 U.S. Congress, *Congressional Record: Proceedings and Debates of the 86th Congress, Second Session*, vol. 106, pt. 1 (Washington, D.C.: Government Printing Office, 1960), 1293–1294, accessed June 6, 2025, https://babel.hathitrust.org/cgi/pt?id=uc1.31210026416923. It is difficult to imagine such a statement being delivered to Congress today.

The government could have saved itself from producing this report if those writing the report had read and believed Psalm 14:3 and Romans 3:10.

As children are trained in righteousness, with their parents acting as God's agents, parents will eventually have the privilege of explaining the gospel of redemption to their children and, by God's grace, may see a new birth. This training in obedience requires instruction in the negative (what is unacceptable behavior), but also what they should be doing instead (the behavior God desires in us).[7]

Notice also that the obedience of Ephesians 6:1 is "in the Lord." *In the Lord* refers to the sphere of pleasing the Lord, and it is two-sided. Children, obey your parents because what they are ask-

> "Whenever there is a conflict between parents and children, it is because one or both are not striving to please the Lord."

ing is pleasing to the Lord. Parents, your instructions to your children are pleasing to the Lord, so children should obey because in doing so they are pleasing the Lord. Consider that whenever there is a conflict between parents and children, it is because one or both are not striving to please the Lord. When the biblical instruction of parents and the obedience of children are functioning as God intended, *this is right.* Or, as Paul states in Colossians 3:20, *this pleases the Lord.*

---

7 On this point, see Priolo, *Teach Them Diligently*, 27-48; Wallace, *For the Love of Discipline*, 71-73; MacArthur, *Successful Christian Parenting*, 113-115, 149.

The command of Ephesians 6:1 is non-negotiable for the *parents*. The responsibility for making this a reality rests squarely on the parents to understand and apply biblical authority and to allow that authority to evolve from the singular authority of parents to occasional, wise, biblical counsel over the span of 16 years or so. Parents will initially be the agents of God, making all moral choices for their children until the children begin to learn about God and develop their own relationship with Him. Eventually, their actions and choices will be driven by a desire to please the Lord rather than their parents, although ideally, as mentioned, there should be little difference.

Both parents and children must learn to differentiate between the commands and principles of Scripture and matters of personal preference.

"Obedience to parents is for a season and is logically replaced by obedience to God."

Parents should give their children increasing responsibility and freedom as they get older, including the freedom to make some choices contrary to the preferences of the parents.[8] Matters of preference should never drive a wedge or cause any significant disagreements between adults. Obedience to parents is for a season and is logically replaced by obedience to God.

I know a Christian man who was in his late 30s when he bought a house for his family. The house need-

---

8 Newheiser and Fitzpatrick, *You Never Stop Being a Parent*, 21-23, 30, 76, 137.

ed a little work, so he set about doing some remodeling. His retired father offered to help out with the project. The new owner decided that the house would be more functional if he removed a wall to make the living room larger (no structural issues were in play). Upon learning of this plan, his father informed him that if this wall was removed, he was done helping his son with the project. The wall came down, and the father was gone. Such conflict should never happen between Christian adults on matters of preference (in this case, the preference was within his own house!).

Chapter 4

Honor Your Father and Mother

Following the instruction for children's obedience in Ephesians 6:1, verse 2 goes on to instruct regarding honor. Honor is a poorly understood term in the present day because it stands in stark contrast to the self-centeredness that defines much of our culture. Honor is the showing of respect or recognition. It is directed toward others. Interestingly, one cannot demand honor, but it is conveyed for deeper reasons of character or position.

Perhaps the United States military forces come closest to demonstrating true honor when brave men and women serve selflessly for love of country and their comrades, often without regard for their own well-being. The command for children to honor father and mother in verse 2 naturally flows from verse 1, as parents exercise biblical authority to nurture their children in learning and applying scriptural truth while helping them develop a personal relationship with God. A right relationship with God

> "There is a season of obedience, but honor continues for a lifetime."

will precipitate a concern for others before self, along with a nonnegotiable commitment to obeying biblical commands. It has been wisely said that there is a season of obedience, but honor continues for a lifetime.[1]

---

1 Tim Challies, "Momentary Obedience, Forever Honor." *Tim Challies,* last modified November 24, 2024, accessed, April 19,

Honor speaks of attitude, while obedience speaks of action. Honor means to value highly, to hold in the highest regard and respect. Concerning the family relationship, this idea was first introduced in the Ten Commandments (see Exodus 20:12, "Honor your father and your mother, that your days may be long in the land that the LORD your God is giving you"). This is the only commandment of the 10 that relates to family, because this one principle alone is enough to secure the right relationship of children to their parents for a lifetime. Not only that, but it is the key principle behind all right human relationships in society. A person who grows up with a sense of respect for and obedience to his parents will have the foundation for honoring the authority of other leaders and the rights of other people in general. Perhaps the greatest deficiency in our society today is the lack of respect—for people in general, for authorities, for human life—and this is because parents have failed to teach children about honor, particularly as applied to their own parents.[2]

Honor also follows position (1 Pet. 2:17). For example, think of the President of the United States, law enforcement officers, and elders in the local church. People in these positions of honor are held in high esteem simply because they occupy the position. This does not mean blind agreement with everything they say or do, but even when there may be disagreement, honor

2025, https://www.challies.com/commandment-we-forgot/momentary-obedience-forever-honor/.

2 John MacArthur, *Ephesians*, MacArthur New Testament Commentary (Chicago: Moody Press, 1986), 311-312.

remains in place. It should be evident that obedience and honor are not the same. Therefore, adult children do not obey without question like they did when they were five years old, and parents should not expect that from their adult children. Adult children can disagree while honoring their parents. As discussed earlier, young adults are now striving to obey God, which is much better than obeying their fallible parents.

What Does Honor Look Like?

Before we consider what honor looks like practically, we must review some essentials to ensure we get this right. Honor cannot be demanded, but goes with the position. Real honor is generated from deep within the heart, and the desire to honor cannot be manufactured. Honoring parents is God's idea, and therefore, when applied rightly, is a very good thing. Consider the Apostle Paul's admonition in 1 Timothy 5:4, where children are directed "to make some return to their parents, for this is pleasing in the sight of God." The idea here is that children owe a debt to those who brought them into the world. This could be financial support, but sometimes it is as simple as giving them the courtesy of interacting with them in their old age. This verse encompasses the idea of showing honor, which could be expressed in many different ways.

Showing honor will look different for various people and their parents, but here is a list of practical actions that will give you a general idea.

1. Tell your parents you love them.

2. Do a chore for your parents. Ideally, you can choose one that your parent dislikes the most and do it without them knowing.

3. Show love to your siblings. Make an effort to get to know and understand each other and get along as much as possible.

4. Take an interest in what your parent is interested in.

5. Listen to your parents' stories (even if you have heard them before). Show an interest in their history.

6. Ask about what life was like when your parents were teenagers.

7. Share stories.

8. Ask your parents for their opinion.

9. Always tell the truth in all your interactions.

10. Never speak disrespectfully, even when you disagree (Prov. 30:17).

11. Speak well of your parents, keeping them in high esteem (Prov. 30:11).

12. Compliment your parents.

13. Find opportunities to serve others with your parents, including them when possible.

14. Always be teachable since your parents' advice might still be useful regardless of their age.

15. Plan time with parents.

16. Bring well-behaved grandchildren to visit their grandparents. While younger children can be

a real blessing, ill-behaved grandchildren (or great-grandchildren) can pose a real threat to elderly adults. The greatest fear of the elderly is falling, so kids who are out of control pose a real threat. If kids are running around, jumping on furniture, and otherwise doing what kids will do on their own, don't bring them along to visit the elderly, simply because the safety risk is too great. Additionally, apply this line of thinking to the church environment.

17. Bring a well-mannered pet for a short visit. Pets can bring enjoyment and comfort if they are well-trained. Unfortunately, most pet owners think their pets are much better behaved than they are and do not realize that most people do not appreciate them like their owners do. Ask permission before showing up with a pet. Instead of asking, "Do you mind if I bring Fido along?" (to which most parents will respond affirmatively, regardless of their true feelings), ask, "I can bring Fido along if you want to see him, but I can also drop him off at my son's house on the way, no problem. Which do you prefer?" There is a big difference in how well-meaning adult children ask a question like this.

18. Help your parents with their personal finances. Be careful here. Offer just enough help, but don't take total control away while they are still capable. Adult children can provide financial support, if needed, following scriptural commands (1 Tim. 5:8).

19. Help your parents with legal documents, such as Power of Attorney, Health Care Directive, and a will or trust.

20. Discuss your parents' wishes for their funeral.

21. Help your parents with cybersecurity issues, thereby safeguarding them from various scams and potential identity theft.

22. Help your parents with vehicle maintenance, or even the purchase of a vehicle if they still drive.

23. Help your parents with home maintenance.

24. Help your parents with their cell phone, iPad, or computer. Much of this is difficult for parents to learn and remember, so be patient.

25. Help parents with their taxes. If you are capable, do their taxes for them or find a reputable tax service.

26. Take your parents out for lunch or to an event they would enjoy. Consider that parents may reach an age when they have outlived all of their friends!

27. Take your parents to church with you.

28. Accompany your parents to medical appointments.

29. Ask your parents about their experiences as veterans.

I must emphasize again that honor might look different in each family, depending on how parents and their adult children interact. Some years ago, as Mother's Day was approaching, I heard a well-meaning Christian leader suggest that everyone who could, should do something nice for their mother, like mowing her grass. Although I appreciate the thought behind the advice, the specifics just would not have worked in our family. My mother is 90 years old, lives alone in her own home, and is very capable and independent. One of her greatest joys in life is cutting her nearly one acre of lawn with her lawn tractor. If I had tried to wrestle that chore away from her, I may well have been excommunicated from the family!

In summary, children, regardless of their age, should recognize their parents' significance in their lives. I realize for some people honoring parents is fraught with difficulty and you may need to humbly and prayerfully wrestle with what that honor could look like in your family situation. Nevertheless, commit to obeying Scripture and do what you can to show honor. Teach your children to do the same by modeling what fulfillment of this biblical command can look like. During the years of raising young children, honor may be way off your radar, but these are the years when honor must be taught and practiced by example. Some years in the future, you will be very glad that your children learned about honor as you are the recipient of those blessings. Remember, always be grateful for your parents and grant grace, because no parent has ever been perfect.

> "Listen to your father who gave you life, and
> do not despise your mother when she is old."
> (Prov. 23:22)

Chapter 5

Gracious Speech

Bill is in his mid-50s and has a best friend who is a good bit younger than he is and is also named Bill. Bill affectionately calls his young friend "Billy." Billy is 25 years old. The two are often asked how they got together, since it is a little different for such good friends to have the age difference of these two men. When asked, these two guys take great joy in telling their story with ever-changing degrees of detail and embellishment. The bottom line is that Billy is actually Bill Jr.—Bill's son!

Ned is a junior at college. He is getting good grades and is on track to graduate in a career field with promising job prospects. Ned has not been home since he came to campus nearly three years ago. He usually tags along with a friend over the holidays and during semester breaks, and he has worked on campus during the summers. Additionally, he has not spoken to his parents since he left for college. When asked by a good friend about his parents and his home life, he stated that his home life was "toxic" and he was never going back.

These two scenarios could not be more different. But why the difference? Perhaps the more important question for parents is: which type of parent do you want to be as your child moves into adulthood. Much of the complex answer to this important question is related to how we communicate—how do we talk to our young adults?

How We Speak

Ephesians 4:29 instructs us, "Let no corrupting talk come out of your mouths, but only such as is good for building up, as fits the occasion, that it may give grace to those who hear." Too often our harshest words are aimed at those we ought to love the most. Christians, in particular, need to be very deliberate about the words they speak. Not only are we instructed to avoid any words that could be categorized as corrupt or unwholesome, but on the positive side, our speech should be building up another person. The words we speak should always be extending grace to the hearer.

Consider these wise words within the context of communicating with our adult children. What is needed to build up another can only be discerned by listening well to another. Don't be the person who has all the answers before you even hear out the concerns of another. Those who want to show sensitivity should listen often and long, and talk short and seldom.[1] If you are going to err in this arena, err by remaining silent. After all, "Even a fool who keeps silent is considered wise; when he closes his lips, he is deemed intelligent" (Prov. 17:28). Your mother's advice could still be applied here: "If you can't say anything nice, don't say anything at all!"

A biblical understanding of authority, obedience, and honor lays the foundation for practical guidance on interactions between parents and their adult children. It's really not that complicated—parents should relate

---

1 J. Oswald Sanders, *Spiritual Leadership* (Chicago, IL: Moody Press, 1994), 75.

to their adult children like they would any other adult. Think about how adults relate to each other in the local church. If we see someone in obvious sin, we lovingly confront them by coming alongside to help. If we want an opinion regarding a matter of preference from someone we respect, we ask for it. Unsolicited opinions are rarely welcome. In fact, the person who is quick to offer their opinion without invitation is typically the last person anyone cares to ask or hear. Welch wisely said:

> "It is almost always unhelpful to give advice to someone who is troubled unless the troubled one asks. Advice is what we would do in another's situation, even though we might never have been in that situation. It typically sounds teacher-like, and it bypasses compassion. It is rarely personal. So hold back your advice unless it is requested."[2]

I understand that this issue is complicated because we are talking about the familial child-parent relationship here, even though the child is technically an adult. Certainly a parent's love is in play here, but often there is more. Sometimes we intervene because we can see the mistake coming and want to save our children from the pain and expense of an error. Here again, our theology must inform our actions. Since we understand that God is sovereign, allow Him to accomplish all good things without your meddling. Sometimes good things include

---

2 Edward T. Welch, *Caring for One Another: 8 Ways to Cultivate Meaningful Relationships* (Wheaton, IL: Crossway, 2018), 47.

short-term failure and pain because that can be the quickest route to learning valuable life lessons. On the other hand, sometimes we intervene because we do not want the personal embarrassment that might come our way because of our adult child's actions. Reputation cannot be our overriding concern without considering the possibility that such consternation has become an idol in our lives.[3]

Advice

After your child is married, you are removed from the potential role of being a primary source of advice in your adult child's life. Now the spouse must fulfill that role. Remember that by God's design, the husband-wife relationship is the primary relationship, and all other human relationships are secondary to it. Especially in the early years of the adult child's marriage, when asked for advice, the wise parent will ask, "Have you talked to your spouse about this?" If they have not, you should direct them back to their spouse without offering your opinion. Remember, our adult children are to be primarily concerned with pleasing their spouses, not their parents (1 Cor. 7:33-34).

> "Remember that they are adults. Treat them as adults. Communicate with them as adults."

---

3 On this point, see Brad Bigney, *Gospel Treason* (Phillipsburg, NJ: P&R Publishing, 2012), 64, 169, 193; Elyse Fitzpatrick, *Idols of the Heart: Learning to Long for God Alone* (Phillipsburg, NJ: P&R Publishing, 2016), 46, 101, 133.

Here is some sound counsel for parents of adult children (applying Prov. 30:32): imagine that you have a piece of duct tape over your mouth. You may only remove the imaginary duct tape to offer advice or counsel when you are asked specifically for that from your adult child. If you are not asked, the duct tape stays in place.[4] I have relayed this simple concept to a number of parents in our local church as their children were preparing for marriage. Many parents have come back later, saying this was the most helpful thing they ever learned about this new phase of their lives. Remember that they are adults. Treat them as adults. Communicate with them as adults.

---

4 Aucoin and Wallace, "Biblical Authority," https://www.faith-lafayette.org/resources/podcast/biblical-authority.

Chapter 6

The Wedding

In addressing the topic of the wedding, I will admit that I feel like a man voluntarily going before the firing squad. Many people have strongly held beliefs about what a wedding should be. The reality is that most of these beliefs are preferences and are, therefore, negotiable. However, a discussion of the wedding is necessary because I have observed this is a frequent place where well-meaning parents insert themselves in unwelcome ways as the young couple prepares to begin their new married life together. Reality entertainment has captured the ugliness of the "mother-of-the-bride-zilla" for entertainment purposes, but unfortunately, such ugliness may also show up in Christian parents. Parents should understand one thing about the wedding—it is not about them, their desires, their preferences, or even their reputations.

The Perfect Wedding

The wedding is all about the bride. I am the father of three sons, but a friend of mine who has two daughters told me that little girls start planning their wedding at around age three. I was shocked! I was pretty sure he was exaggerating, so I began asking young brides-to-be during our premarital counseling sessions if this was, in fact, true. To my amazement, I have yet to find the bride-to-be where this was not the case.

Given how much time and care the bride has poured into planning, it's wise to acknowledge that her hopes and plans for this day are more deeply rooted than anyone else's. Parental wishes and expectations should all be set aside. Concerns about reputation and family traditions should find another outlet. The wedding day is about the bride, for the bride, and should fulfill, as nearly as possible, what she has been envisioning for years. This is not to say that she should not consider traditions or the wishes of others in the family, but in the end, she holds the final veto power and can and should make her wedding what she wants it to be.

I know of one young couple who were so beleaguered by parental demands about their wedding that they secretly eloped and were married. Some time later, after all the onerous plans of the parents were in place, they went through the wedding ceremony with no one the wiser that they had already been married for months. Parents, please don't drive your children to this kind of action.

The Biblical Wedding

Does the concept of a "biblical wedding" exist? I have known parents who try to muscle their preferences into the wedding ceremony under the guise of the necessity of a "biblical wedding." While there is no prescription for a biblical wedding in Scripture, the Bible is clear on what marriage is intended to be. It is clear that marriage is meant to be a covenant between one man and one woman for life. In Bible times, it was a common practice for there to be a celebration and ceremony for the wedding couple, sometimes lasting many days (John 2:1-12, Matt. 25:1-13). Besides the ceremony, the most important aspect of the wedding festivities was (and is today) the exchange of the vows, the promise and the covenant.

When we look at the biblical record, we find that God established marriage in the beginning. Marriage is God's idea. The first marriage was based on a covenant promise and inaugurated a new and primary responsibility and relationship (Gen. 2:24). All other human relationships are secondary to what God has designed in marriage. The essence of marriage consists of three actions: leaving, cleaving, and becoming one flesh. Marriage vows, in whatever form they are expressed, should express the following biblical truths (adapted from Adam Burell).[1]

For the Man:

- It is a promise to love his wife as Christ loved the church (Eph. 5:25)
- It is a promise to live sacrificially for his wife (Eph. 5:25)
- It is a promise to lead his wife spiritually (Eph. 5:26)
- It is a promise to leave his parents and cleave alone to his wife (Eph. 5:31)
- It is a promise of monogamy (1 Cor. 7, Heb. 13:4)

---

1 Adam Burrell, "What Constitutes a Biblical Marriage?" *G3 Ministries*, last modified February 7, 2022, accessed May 2, 2025, https://g3min.org/what-constitutes-a-biblical-marriage/.

For the Woman:

- It is a promise to joyfully submit to her husband (Eph. 5:22)

- It is a promise to respect her husband (Eph. 5:31)

- It is a promise to leave her parents and cleave alone to her husband (by implication in Eph. 5:31)

- It is a promise of monogamy (1 Cor. 7, Heb. 13:4)

Ironically, well-meaning parents usurping control of the wedding directly oppose the concept of leaving and cleaving. More than once, I have offered that only two things must come out of the wedding ceremony: first, at end of the day, they must be legally married, and secondly, as much as possible, the wedding itself brings glory to God. I prefer to see a text like Ephesians 5:22-33 used to show how God has designed marriage to reflect the relationship of Christ and His church. But the music, the colors, the flowers, the attendants, etc., are all matters of preference under the purview of the bride. It is right and good that the new couple be married, if possible, by and among those who love and cherish marriage, who will assist them in the responsibilities of married life, and who will remind them both of the seriousness of marriage and its blessings. The reality is that all other matters of preference that cause such angst during wedding planning are soon forgotten and fade away into history.

Parents' Roles

Weddings can be incredibly expensive, but need not be so. The "bride's day in the bride's way" counsel suggested above must be tempered with the financial realities of each individual situation. The tradition of the bride's parents paying for the wedding is gradually becoming a thing of the past, and that's probably a good thing. If the parents assist at all in the cost of the wedding, the contributed amount should be specified upfront so the bride can make her plans within the financial constraints that exist. Under no circumstances should financing of the wedding be used to hold the bride hostage to the wishes of the parents.

The true character of parents and their adult children will be revealed during the stress of all that goes into a wedding. Let me be very clear—these issues are not simply my opinions. Those who are enslaved to a self-focused heart will have the biggest challenge in leaving the bulk of the decisions in the hands of the bride-to-be (Jer. 17:9). From a theological viewpoint, the bottom-line issue in play is idolatry. Consider the definition of idolatry offered by Bigney: "An idol is anything or anyone that captures our hearts, minds, and affections more than God."[2] If you simply must have your child's wedding conducted in a certain way that has no biblical basis, and you will do whatever it takes to make that happen, you are an idolater!

Parents can be invaluable assets to the bride in the days and months leading up to the wedding, but only if they communicate well and recognize their supporting role from the outset. Consider the following statements conveyed by the parents to the bride:

---

2 Bigney, *Gospel Treason*, 24.

- This is your day. Let me know what I can do to help.

- Here is the financial support that we can offer for your wedding. Use it as you want.

- I am not going to pester you about any details or timelines, but again, I'll help wherever you want me to.

- As soon as you have decided on the size of your wedding, the venue, and the guest list, let me know so I have a feel for what to expect.

- We are very excited for your special day and offer our unwavering support.

I know that this counsel will be extremely difficult for some parents to accept and even more difficult to implement. However, remember these facts: this young, soon-to-be-wed couple is composed of two adults. You must now view them as your equals and your approach to the

> "If you simply must have your child's wedding conducted in a certain way that has no biblical basis, and you will do whatever it takes to make that happen, you are an idolater!"

wedding is setting the stage for your relationship with them for many decades into the future. This is not about you (Rom. 12:3). Additionally, remember that you have trained them to make good, God-honoring decisions, and now it is time to entrust them to God as they do just that.

The Spouse

What about a child's choice of a future spouse? The criteria for selecting a godly spouse are issues that should have been taught by the parents and the church long before an engagement is on the horizon. I agree with Newheiser and Fitzpatrick that if you don't have your child's heart, you will have little influence in the choice of a spouse, regardless of your understanding of your authority (or lack thereof). Furthermore, any promises made when the child was younger is unlikely to hold any weight.[3] The ideal is that young people marry with the blessing of their parents, but parents must recognize that their adult children have the right to choose their own life partners, and their parents do not have veto power over this decision.[4]

---

3 Newheiser and Fitzpatrick, *You Never Stop Being a Parent*, 140.

4 Concerning situations where an adult child is considering marrying an unbeliever, see Question 17 on pages 111-112.

Chapter 7

Adult Children in the Home

By the early 1990s, 55 percent of adults ages 18-24 were living with parents. Today, one in three adults ages 18-34 lives in their parents' home.[1] While some might rationalize this trend as a result of economic realities or another oversimplification, our biblical worldview should cause us to peel back the layers to discern the underlying cause for this behavior. This situation has become so commonplace that you likely know a family in this situation, or you yourself are in the midst of it. The reasons vary: career or marriage difficulties, or some have never left home after completing their secondary education.

Faced with such situations, some parents just try to survive day to day with their adult child in the house, hoping that magically, one day things will change. This is unlikely to occur. Recall my working definition of the goal of parenting from an earlier chapter: *The goal of Christian parenting is to raise up adults who know the God of the Bible and are prepared to interact with their culture from a biblical worldview while being fully independent and functional.* When your adult children are living at home, the two key areas where you can still support them—based on this definition—are helping them become functional and independent. Sadly, the foundational goals of knowing God and developing that biblical

---

1 David Burggraff and Lucy Burggraff, "Parenting Your Adult Children," paper presented at The Shepherds 360 Church Leaders Conference, Cary NC, October 16-18, 2023.

worldview are best accomplished during their younger formative years and are less likely to occur seamlessly as parents try to relate to their young adult.

Being Functional

If your adult child is living at home and is not working, or they are working but are not making a living wage, they are not functional today. Parents can help here, although the biblical concepts of hard work and its link to prosperity would have ideally been taught while the child was younger. Now, in the case of a young adult, the parent is in the mode of making up for lost time in helping adult children develop a godly work ethic and acquiring marketable skills so that their labor will be in high demand so they can "stand before kings" (Prov. 22:29).

Parents have a God-ordained responsibility to avoid supporting their kids' misbehavior and laziness.[2] You must recognize that the most loving thing you can do for this young person is to help them investigate options and then provide an adequate incentive to ensure they follow through with a plan to achieve functional independence.

The incentive piece of this is simply some version of: "You can live here if you are pursuing some type of training or are otherwise progressing in your work toward independence. If you don't want to do that, you need to leave." The options I am connecting to function are some types of training (school, apprenticeship, or

---

2 Newheiser and Fitzpatrick, *You Never Stop Being a Parent*, 72-73.

on-the-job) that will make them employable, where they can earn a living wage—a wage that will provide them with the resources to live independently. Essentially, you are telling your young adult that "you will not be allowed to live and act like a child in this home. You are an adult, and you must now act like an adult."

Too many young adults find remaining in childhood a rather comfortable setting, and really do need a little extra push into reality (2 Thess. 3:10-12). Parents cannot enable irresponsible behavior by their adult children. In the Western world, we presently live in a culture where people, in general, do not want to work. Christian parents must obey the clear commands and principles of Scripture by ensuring their adult children are acting as reasonable, functional adults. All adults have choices, and this is an issue where your adult child must make a choice. The choice to continue living irresponsibly will mean they need to leave your home.[3]

All of our children have grown up in a materialistic culture where accumulating things is the default purpose of life. The mantra of "you can have it now" with no concern about paying for it has been too readily adopted, even by many Christians. The Bible has much to say about money and how we use it. Consider the truth that our use of (and attitude toward) money reveals our heart and what we worship. We desperately need biblical wisdom to use money the way God intended. If your adult child struggles with the misuse of money and

---

3 Concerning the difficult conversation of having to tell a child they are no longer welcome in the house, see Question 18 on page 112.

debt, someone intervening to pay off their debt is merely treating a symptom. In such cases, I recommend focused biblical counseling on God's principles for managing money, coupled with the expectation that they take responsibility for paying off their own debts.

These heart-to-heart discussions with your adult child may include talking about their long-held dreams. Here I am thinking about things like being a movie producer, ballet star, or professional athlete. While a few individuals make a living as professionals in these fields, many more dream of these activities but will never rise to the level of making a living while pursuing them. Young people must understand that at some point, their dreams can be pursued as a hobby, but they need to understand the reality that they will never make a living by pursuing that dream. Parents can help their adult children face these facts and move ahead with life.

I was recently talking to the owner of a plumbing company about some work we needed done in our church building. The conversation turned to his difficulties in getting and keeping employees. He confided that he was at the point where he would hire anyone who would just show up to work on time every day. He was willing to teach them everything else. I share this account to emphasize that the problem isn't a lack of well-paying jobs. The deeper issue is that we've largely raised a generation more inclined to play than to work—and enabling parents have only made matters worse.

Being Independent

The parental efforts at helping a young adult become functional are closely tied to the tangible goal of independence. Young adults must achieve the ability to live on their own, in their own residence, and be able to cover all of their own living expenses. Anything less places undue hardship on parents and society, and stunts the young adult's growth and maturity. Parents, we love our children. But sheltering them from becoming functional and independent is not real love. It is helpful to establish some time frames and realistic check points for goals related to functionality and independence. A well-defined target is always much easier to hit. It may also be helpful to charge your young adult room and board to help them adopt a realistic view of life. Living is not free!

An example might be helpful. Suppose you have a 22-year-old son who dropped out of an electrical engineering program in college after two years. He floated around for a year after that and has now landed back at home. Your assistance in nudging him toward independence might steer him toward the 2-year electrician program at the local technical school, along with summer employment as a laborer with an electrical contractor. He can live at home while he completes the program, paying you a modest monthly room and board, and then you expect him to become gainfully employed with an electric company, and be out of your house 4 months after graduation. In such a situation, he is expected to pay his own tuition and work while he is going to school. He is responsible for his own transportation costs, including car insurance, if applicable. The rules and schedule are clear, and it is all very reasonable and attainable. The clarity of these expectations has been ensured by putting them all in writing, discussing them with your young adult, and then having the parents and young adult sign them. This may seem like overkill, but this process is necessary to solidify these expectations in everyone's thinking. At this point, he can choose to make it work or not. If not, he can find other living arrangements.

Thus far, this discussion assumes your young adult is capable, although likely lacking motivation. There are cases where young adults have true developmental or physical limitations. Such circumstances may require some extra time and guidance for the right kind of training, but ideally, the end results can still be achieved.[4]

We had one son who had a couple of "false starts" with employment after college and ended up at home with nothing to show for several years of work. We welcomed him into our home with some conditions that looked something like the following:

1. You are going to find a job. Until you are employed, finding a job will be your job, and you will spend 8 hours each day looking for work, applying for jobs, interviewing, etc.

2. Our house rules apply—quiet hours, meal times, etc. You'll be expected to accompany us when we attend church services.

3. You are a guest here. We love you, but your parents are in charge, and we will modify any

---

4 For more on parenting young adults with limitations, see Question 16 on page 111.

house rules as needed when we see that changes
need to be made.

There may have been several additional stipulations that
I can no longer recall, but our approach made it obvious that this was not a vacation at a country club with
no responsibilities. I had our son sign the written rules
to ensure he understood our expectations. As I review
these now, I will admit that they do bear some resem-
blance to what might be posted on the gate of the state
penitentiary!

Within a few days, he had a job working construc-
tion, and within a few weeks, he had employment related
to his college major. From there, he has proceeded on a
positive career track for the past 18 years. My point in
offering this example is that you know your young adult
and you know what might be required to provide the
needed motivation. I am sure my methods in this example were not perfect, but by God's grace, they worked. By
the way, we have a good relationship with this son and
his family, and he presently serves as a vice-president
in a nationally-known company. So, although the rules
may have seemed harsh at the time, they did not damage
the relationship long-term.

"I Need a Year Off"

What about "taking a year off?" It's increasingly common
for young adults to want to "take a year off"—whether
between high school and further education, during their
training years, or even after completing training, before
entering the workforce. This is a big mistake! Too often,

these young adults never return to complete the original plan, or if they do, they have squandered what should have been a productive year. Furthermore, they leave an unimpressive gap in school or employment records that could potentially tarnish their reputation in the world of employment.

Seriously consider that God has allotted to each person a discreet number of days of life (Ps. 139:16), and the Bible consistently conveys the idea that God expects us to use these days wisely. Further, Proverbs admonishes us to consider the untiring, relentless work of the ant, and to emulate this in our own lives (Prov. 6:6-11). Ants do not take a year off!

Although loving parents can sometimes be convinced of "time off" for their hard-working young adults, the bigger picture of the theology of work cannot justify this action (2 Thess. 3:6-12). Work is not a punishment, but a pre-Fall good part of God's creation. It is not to be avoided, but to be embraced as a good part of life. This is an arena where parents need to help their young adults grow up (1 Cor. 13:11). As a personal anecdote, I have observed that in most cases, "time off" merely results in establishing bad habits and irresponsibility, while living at another's expense. God made us tremendously resilient people, and parents should insist that their young adults function this way.

Expectations

A few additional thoughts on reasonable expectations that parents should have for young adults living in their home that might prove helpful. Everyone should understand that this is not a "normal" situation, and your primary concern is helping them get back on the right track. Too often, the basic issue is that our young adult children want full adult privileges and freedoms without assuming adult responsibilities.[5] This is flawed thinking which must be corrected if parents are going to help in any meaningful way. As parents, by having adult children living in your home, you are making a short-term accommodation that must be linked with a change in their thinking and behavior.

Parents in this situation should require that their adult child:

- Keep their room clean to the parents' standards
- Pay rent
- Take responsibility for household chores
- Maintain open and honest communication
- Progress toward the goals of functional and independent
- Keep quiet hours
- Keep rules, particularly respecting your moral values (sex, drugs, alcohol, etc.)
- Communicate about their schedule
- Do their own laundry
- Pay their bills on time
- Repay debts

---

5 Newheiser and Fitzpatrick, *You Never Stop Being a Parent*, 70.

- Generally, understand that they are a guest in this home
- Understand that this is a short-term accommodation, with some projected end dates

Moral Standards

It's important to take a closer look at the moral standards that ought to be upheld in the home. As a Christian, the moral standards of the home must never be compromised. Consider the Old Testament account of Eli the priest and his sons. Eli's sons were vile and went through the motions of the priesthood for their own benefit, but they did not know God (1 Sam. 2-3). Eli admonished them verbally, but that was all. The Law required stoning for their actions (Deut. 21:18-21). In 1 Samuel 3:29, God pinpoints Eli's problem in addressing his sons and

> "Wise parents realize that physical, emotional, and financial resources always have limits."

their sin: "*You* honor your sons above me."

If the adult children in your home refuse to live within the moral standards of your home, verbal cajoling is not the correct response. The only correct response to these actions is that they need to leave. As Newheiser and Fitzpatrick state, "When dad and mom, like Eli, become enablers of a sinful lifestyle, they inadvertently dishonor the Lord and share in the sin and guilt of their kids, even though that's the farthest thing from their minds."[6] Many parents know full well the ongoing moral failures of their children living in their home, but refuse to address the situation. The excuses are many: hoping things will change, extending grace and love to their child, giving them more time, not wanting to face conflict, or fear of driving them away and suffering loss. However, there is really one simple question that parents must answer: who will we love and honor more, God or our wayward child? Remember the words of Joshua to the people of Israel: " . . . choose this day whom you will serve, . . . But as for me and my house, we will serve the Lord" (Josh. 24:15).

Even when our children are non-believers, through God's common grace, they can learn to be independent and productive in our society. Parents should still be as supportive as possible in many areas of the unbelieving adult child's life. But these parents must never lower their moral standards and thereby compromise their own beliefs. Remember, we must honor God more than we honor our children. To do otherwise is idolatry.

For some parents, their own physical, emotional, or financial health will be strained in untenable ways if an adult child moves back home. If this is the case, the young adult cannot live in the parents' home. An understanding relative may be able to help in some cases, but regardless, parents are not responsible for providing in

---

6 Newheiser and Fitzpatrick, *You Never Stop Being a Parent*, 61.

these cases. Wise parents realize that physical, emotional, and financial resources always have limits.[7]

---

7 Gary Chapman and Ross Campbell, *Your New Life with Adult Children* (Chicago, IL: Moody Publishers, 2024), 115.

Chapter 8

Becoming Friends

Glenda has a standing coffee date with her best friend every Tuesday morning at 9 AM. She guards this appointment with the resolve of a mother hen guarding her chicks. She takes this approach because this time is so precious and enjoyable for her and her best friend. Although her friend Ginny is a good bit younger than Glenda, they use this time to share recent events, catch up on family matters, and pray for each other. It is the sweetest of times that most women dream of, but is all too rare. Oh, did I mention that Ginny is Glenda's daughter?

While it is essential that parents of young children realize that their children don't need them to be a friend—the children need a parent not a friend in the younger years—after your children become adults, ideally you will have the privilege of becoming their friend. When your children were young, you were the in-control parents, and your young ones were the in-submission children. During the training process, parents should have learned to gradually relinquish hands-on control as their children developed the capacity for wise decision-making and independence.

The healthy view of adult children is that they now become respected friends with their parents. It should be obvious that this can only happen in the absence of the command-and-control mindset of the parents. Consider: if you were not the parent of your adult children, would they still want to be your friend? This should be our goal as parents of these young adults. For the discussion in this chapter, let's assume your son or daughter has married and may have their own children. If they are single, many of these principles still apply with some obvious exclusions.

Just Like Your Own

When your son or daughter marries, adopt your son-in-law or daughter-in-law as one of your own. There should no longer be any difference between your own adult child and the one they have married. Treat them as your own when you call, when you visit in person, and when you give gifts. Make them feel a part of your family by inviting them to participate in family activities and decisions. Celebrate them the same as you do your own child for birthdays and other special events, always showing the same love and attention you give your own child. By your actions, you have gained another adult child and friend by way of this marriage.

I have typically been an abysmal failure in celebrating birthdays, anniversaries, and other special days. Thankfully, my wife makes up for my deficiencies in this realm. We have three daughters-in-law that we love as our own. Many years ago, my wife started recognizing them on Mother's Day, just to let them know that we thought they were very special, being the mothers of our grandchildren. As a clueless male, it never would have occurred to me to celebrate with them in this way. For years, I was challenged to remember my own mother on Mother's Day! By a simple act like this, we can tangibly demonstrate that they are as much a part of our family as our own sons.

To Leave and Cleave

Help your married children leave and cleave (Gen. 2:24; Mark 10:7; Matt. 19:5). Stand beside the new husband and wife, not between them. They should know that pleasing their spouse comes way before pleasing you as their parent. God's design has always been that the husband-wife relationship is the priority, and all other relationships are secondary to it. As a Christian, you certainly agree with this concept, but you must also put it into action.

From an earlier chapter, remember that adult children are *adults,* and you should always treat them like any other adult friends in your life. Practically, this means you can offer advice when asked, but you never give orders as if you were the general of

> "Stand beside the new husband and wife, not between them."

the family while they were some lower-ranking enlisted servants. If a son or daughter asks for your advice, you should make sure they have consulted their spouse first, especially during their earlier years of marriage. If you, as a parent, have always been the number one go-to person for advice, this shift will take some practice, but you must ensure that it happens. To do otherwise is to deviate from God's ways in marriage. If you violate God's plan for marriage in this realm, be assured your behavior is destructive, causing unnecessary heartache and hardship!

It is essential to allow your adult children to develop their own family identity and decision-making process. How might this look practically? If you are planning a family trip, you can invite them to join you, but you should never guilt them into participating. You should not even require a reason if they choose to decline your invitation.

I know of one young man who is an executive at a prestigious accounting firm. His in-laws planned an exotic vacation and made all the plans, assuming all of their adult children and in-laws would jump at the opportunity to join them. The event was scheduled for the first two weeks of April, and everything was in place before any of the adult children were notified. Bowing to family pressure, the young man grudgingly went on vacation. The two weeks in April preceding the April 15 tax deadline were the busiest of the year with "all hands on deck" at his accounting firm. While on this "vacation," he was even unsure if his career was in peril because of the poor timing of this event. This kind of family tension and drama could easily have been avoided if the parents had simply treated their adult children as adults.

They Are Mature Adults

If parents are going to establish a friend-to-friend bond with their adult children, they must treat their children as adults in all areas of life. Again, the best advice for parents is to "mind your own business" unless you are asked for an opinion. If you are asked, give it graciously without being judgmental or coercive in any way. Becoming friends with your adult children is a prize to be sought after by parents, but it won't happen without deliberate attitudes and actions.

Another essential step for parents who want to build a friendship with their adult children is to avoid any form of controlling behavior. I know parents who are overly controlling, even though they are doing what they do "out of love." It has been wisely said, regarding your adult children, this is the time "to love them with open arms." Parents can be overly controlling by worrying—there is no need to check up on them continually. They are old enough now to take care of all the needs in their lives. This is a time to trust God's sovereignty over their lives. Parents must also avoid second-guessing their adult children's decisions. This includes all financial decisions, career choices, where to live, politics, and when or how many children to have.

I know one grandfather who had an unwelcome, trite response every time he learned he had another grandchild on the way. His quip was, "Those who play have to pay!" While I assume he thought this was a fine joke, I know that the newly expectant parents did not appreciate his attempt at humor. Remember, parents have the privilege of standing alongside their adult children, providing support in a way few other people can, but always with mutual respect as they relate to each other as adults.

Matters of Preference

Finally, remember that much of what goes on in all of our lives is a matter of preference. Parents must respect their adult children's preferences. This is where parents' preferences and traditions must be set aside, and adult children can make their own choices. Holidays are a great example to consider. Many families have their holiday traditions, but a newly married couple might now have two competing sets of traditions to choose from, sometimes occurring simultaneously. Or, they may opt to establish new traditions unlike what either the husband or wife knew earlier in their lives. These are all matters of preference. Let me state the obvious—no one can be dogmatic about traditions. Traditions and preferences do not carry the weight of the Holy Scriptures, even though some people act like they do!

Everyone likes to spend time with their friends. If parents can establish this kind of friend relationship with their adult children, both will want to spend time together, enjoying it immensely. And most importantly, the relationship will be conducted the way God designed.

Chapter 9

Grandchildren

Grandchildren are one of life's greatest blessings and joys. My wife is frequently awestruck by how I relate to my grandchildren compared to how I related to our own sons many years ago. Apparently, my sons say the same thing. And I will admit, it is different. I enjoy having these little grandsons crawl all over me while I am on my back with my head under the kitchen sink attempting a repair. I am amused as they dig through my tools, thinking these are the greatest treasures ever. Something has definitely changed, and I can only define that change as "I became a grandparent!"

While grandparents are enjoying these little blessings, we must remember some truths that are much easier to recite than to live out. Let's be

> **"The role of grandparent is very different than the role of parent."**

clear: the role of grandparent is very different than the role of parent.

Who is Responsible?

Grandparents are not responsible for raising their grandchildren. While grandparents typically love being involved in the lives of their grandchildren, they are not responsible for them. This means they do not discipline them, train them, feed them, clothe them, care for them, educate them, or function as primary caregivers in any other way.

"Wait a minute!" you say. "I love buying clothes for my grandkids, and I am certainly going to feed them when they visit." Of course you are. The point here is that you are not taking on the role of the parent in any of these areas, and you are never going against the wishes of the parent. You can buy clothes, but only in the style and quantity approved by the parents. You might be thinking, "That's a little strict." But consider the granddaughter who is masterful at talking Grandma into buying certain clothes that she knows her mother will not approve of. Now conflict has been created between mom and grandmother while the daughter has successfully circumvented her mother's directive.

Good communication between parents and grandparents can prevent the potential problems I am trying to highlight. Again, parents are responsible for every aspect of their children's lives with grandparents playing a supporting role that must always be approved by the parents. For example, it is likely that parents will not discipline their children in the same way they were disciplined when they were children. This is not a topic that is open for discussion unless the young parents ask the grandparents for their thoughts (remember the duct tape rule). The same applies in areas of entertainment, food, social activities, and every other aspect of life. It's really not as difficult as it might sound. Grandparents must learn to do what aligns with the parents' wishes for their grandchildren. This is not open to ongoing debate.

Sometimes parents avoid being responsible by using the grandparents. An example of this might be dropping off the grandkids frequently without notice and with the implicit attitude of "do whatever you want." This kind of behavior must be lovingly confronted—and grandparents are in a key position to do so. Parents must become responsible as parents, and enabling behavior by grandparents is not helpful. As much as possible, visits should be scheduled with a clear structure around duration and activities.

Obviously the details will vary among families, but I am attempting to highlight cases where irresponsible parents are taking advantage of grandparents as free and convenient childcare on demand. I heard of one extreme case where the grandparents called the parents to ask if the parents could take *back* their children for the night so the grandparents could go out for the evening! Talk about a role reversal.

Some Practical Thoughts

Should grandparents provide daycare for their grandchildren? This is probably not the best option for most grandparents or their grandchildren for three reasons: (1) grandparents may not be physically able to provide the needed care, (2) parents may take advantage of grandparents in the realm of childcare, and (3) if you, as a grandparent, are a primary daycare provider, you sacrifice a more desirable role as simply a grandparent.

Grandparents must face the fact that they are not as young as they were when they had children, and parenting young children takes a lot of energy. This can be a serious health and safety issue for both grandparents and grandchildren. Perhaps the physical requirements of on-going daycare are too much for the well-meaning grandparent. That bad back simply cannot endure lifting that baby like it did those many years ago. Additionally, the toddler who has now learned to move fast may be in serious danger if the grandparent is a little slow in response. I know of one extreme case where great-grandparents in their late 80s routinely watched their great-granddaughter for one afternoon each week. I was shocked to hear that, during a visit to the local park, they struggled to respond quickly when the

> "Grandparents must face the fact that they are not as young as they were when they had children, and parenting young children takes a lot of energy."

child ran from the playground toward the street. Whereas a parent's quick run to keep the child out of a busy street might seem simple to a younger adult, it is not as easy for the older grandparents. And it is irresponsible to put a grandparent or grandchild in such a situation.

How can a grandparent know if they are being taken advantage of by their adult children? This can be difficult to discern because most grandparents would "do anything" for their beloved grandchildren. Nonetheless, it does happen. Here are a few warning signs that this might be an issue:

- Parents have no backup plan if you (grandparents) are unavailable to provide child care.

- Parents react negatively if you decline to help with childcare.

- You routinely miss your own medical appointments and are rescheduling other commitments so you can do last-minute child care.

- You are frequently dealing with illnesses you contracted from your sick grandchildren while providing childcare.

- You are unable to honor your own parents (see Chapter 4) because of childcare duties.

- You prioritize childcare over ministry in the local church.

- You are unable to fulfill your ministry in the local church due to childcare duties.

- You are physically fatigued because of childcare duties.

If you have read this far in this chapter and you are a grandmother, you are likely thinking, "That's not me!" I encourage you to ask your pastor or another trusted, mature Christian who knows you well if this may be a possible issue in your life. This is not always easy to discern clearly, and it varies for everyone. However, your physical, emotional, and spiritual health are at risk, so it is imperative that you get this right.

The Uniqueness of Grandparents

Finally, it is essential to acknowledge that the roles of child care provider and grandparent are distinct, and if you assume the former, you will inevitably sacrifice some aspects of the latter. Grandparents are unique in that they typically have the time and child-rearing experience to enjoy these little ones in ways parents cannot. It is a great blessing to be able to enjoy all that grandchildren bring without the exhausting responsibilities of parenting. There is good reason why the Bible refers to grandchildren as "the crown of the aged" (Prov. 17:6).

The Book of Proverbs gives us further insights about our God-ordained roles as we age: "The honor of young men is their strength, and the majesty of old men is their gray hair" (Prov. 20:29). The point is simply that as grandparent-aged adults, we are not just parental figures with a few additional years tacked on. We function differently. We view things differently. We are wiser. We have more time. We are more apt to sort our priorities rightly. We should think more consistently in biblical terms. And we can offer our grandchildren the wisdom gained from many decades. For grandparents who are trying to function as parents (even by helping with grandchildren), you may be missing out on how this stage of life, by God's design, is to be different.

In some cases, grandparents take on the role of permanent parenthood again due to a tragedy or abandonment by the parents. I have high regard for grandparents who are able to fulfill this difficult role, and I believe God can grant his strength and grace to face these difficult circumstances. However, this kind of situation should always be understood as the exception rather than the norm. Grandparents should always seek the best for the child in these situations. If grandparents cannot provide the level of care and training needed for any reason, other options should be considered for the welfare of the child.[1]

> "Grandchildren are the crown of the aged,
> and the glory of children is their fathers"
> (Prov. 17:6).

---

1 On the issue of grandparents helping raise their grandchildren, see Question 20 on page 113.

Chapter 10

Being a Purposeful Guest

Picture the following scenario. A young family has a very active household. Five children, aged one to eight, means there is nonstop activity. Mom stays at home and is continually providing meals, changing diapers, doing laundry, homeschooling, taking trips to the library and sporting events for the older kids, and also has several younger moms she ministers to from her church. Dad works full-time, which typically means well over 40 hours per week, including one or two evening meetings each week. Additionally, they try to minister to families from the church in their home once or twice each month. This is a bustling household, but they make it work. Perhaps as a more mature adult, you remember those days well and wonder, "How did we ever do it?"

A Serving Guest

As grandparents, of course you want to visit this family. They live six hours away, so visits mean you are going to be there for a few days, maybe even many days. To make your visit one that is welcomed by the young family and minimizes the disruption to their "normal" life that it could cause, consider the following:

- Ask what dates might work for a visit rather than informing or demanding.
- Ask what you can bring to make the visit easier or to provide something they don't have access to. We

have a daughter-in-law we've been able to bring some favorite baking supplies to—things she can't get where they live. We also frequently try to bring some food items to grill. The grandkids have come to love the sausage links that we bring for breakfast.

- While you are there, provide some child care to make mom's days easier. Maybe your adult kids can even have a date night without children.

- Do a project around the house for them (with their approval). This would be something that would make a needed improvement, but they just don't have the time to get done. Paint a room, fix a leaky faucet, or fix a kitchen drawer. If you don't have such skills, find a handyman and pay them to make the improvement.

- Take over or help with some household duties. Cook a meal, do some laundry, change a diaper. I frequently cook while at my kids' house, but I always get clearance to do so from the "head chef."

- Read some books with the grandkids or take them to the park.

- Offer to go shopping, sparing mom an extra chore.

- Do not expect this family to wait on you or cater to your every need. They are plenty busy!

- Do not expect this family to drop everything to entertain you or schedule special events for you every day.

- Adjust your usual schedule to theirs for meal times, bed time, and wake up time, assuming you are staying in their house.

- If adjusting your schedule is difficult, you need some additional quiet time, or your presence makes the house too crowded, stay at a nearby hotel rather than at their house.

- Do everything you can so the young family enjoys your visit rather than counting down the minutes until you leave. Be a blessing to their household, not a burden.

- Ensure all conversation with the parents is adult-to-adult.

- Never be dogmatic on issues of preference.

- Avoid "hot button" topics where you know you disagree if it will not be discussed in a peaceful manner.

- Have fun, but also remember that daily life is still happening at full speed for this family and will be doing so after you leave.

You can measure the success of your visit by discerning whether they truly hate to see you leave or are breathing a collective sigh of relief that you're finally gone!

After looking through the previous list, perhaps you're thinking, "That doesn't sound like much of a relaxing visit to me. If all I was going to do is work, I could have stayed home!" Consider that Christ himself is the supreme example for us in that He "came not to be served but to serve" (Matt. 20:28). I am not really talking about work here as much as I am talking about serving those you love. Additionally, Acts 20:35 encourages us to "remember the words of the Lord Jesus, how he himself said, 'It is more blessed to give than to receive.'"

Let me encourage you that this service to your young adults will look different for everyone. Perhaps my list of ideas will never apply to your situation, but the biblical pattern of serving others rather than being served must ring true for every disciple of Christ. I pray that you will find the appropriate way to make this practical application.

> "The biblical pattern of serving others rather than being served must ring true for every disciple of Christ."

Chapter 11

Favoritism

Fred and Linda are in their 80s and are well off financially. They have three adult children and have been able to help them with life issues over the years. Sam is the eldest and has pretty much been functional and independent since college. He has three children and they are well on their way to being productive members of society. Siri is the second oldest and has never married. She has had medical issues her entire adult life after dropping out of college. Fred and Linda have given her in excess of $100,000 over the years, and she would be considered barely functional in society. Seth is the youngest, and life never really got going for him. He lives near his parents and regularly receives money from them to support his day-to-day living, since he does not have a regular job. He often eats meals at their house and is the epitome of the adult who never grew up. Fred and Linda also own a large tract of recreational land. Sam believes he is entitled to this property because he has received very little financially from his parents during adulthood, especially compared to his siblings. What do you think? Should Sam receive the recreational property to "even the score" with his siblings, or not?

Most people believe they have a good sense of what is fair and just. However, when we examine this thought theologically, we realize that we are all biased in our understanding of fairness and justice. Only God has the corner on this market. He is perfectly fair and perfectly just. Only as we draw near to Him will our understanding of fairness and justice move closer to reality. This truth should help us understand that we must be humble as we seek to grasp fairness and justice, since our perceptions will always be less than perfect. We will all do well to remember, "Man looks on the outward appearance, but the LORD looks on the heart" (1 Sam. 16:7).

Being Fair and Avoiding Partiality

Perhaps the quickest way to drive a wedge between parents and children (or grandchildren) is to show favoritism. While it is impossible to treat everyone the same in all circumstances, parents and grandparents should make deliberate efforts to accomplish fair and equitable treatment as much as possible. Genuine love dictates that this is the only proper course of action. Those who deliberately receive less or otherwise come up short are sure to notice, and negative feelings will result and persist for a long time.

> "Perhaps the quickest way to drive a wedge between parents and children (or grandchildren) is to show favoritism."

Avoiding favoritism is more than just a good practice in life. Scripture also condemns favoritism as the sin of partiality (James 2:1-9). It is easy for all of us to develop favorites. One good reason to guard against preferential treatment is the theological reality that God brings every person we come across into our lives for His purposes. If we are stumbling through life blinded by the sin of partiality, we will miss out on what God is doing in our lives.

Some years ago, an elderly man from our church was doing yard work on a Saturday afternoon outside the church near a frequently used walking path. Two women came walking by, and he struck up a pleasant conversation with them. Before they parted ways, he told them that this meeting today was appointed by God and he invited them to church the next day. One of the ladies came the next day, became a church member shortly thereafter, and was an active part of the church for the next 15 years. This gentleman was committed to engaging everyone God brought his way in a conversation about Christ! How important that we all avoid the sin of partiality, realizing that we are God's instruments to be used in the lives of others as he sees fit.

Parents and grandparents, avoid the sin of partiality by trying to spend equivalent time with each child. Give gifts that approximate the same value. Communicate in similar ways and with similar frequencies. If stepchildren or adopted children are in the picture, make sure they are treated the same as all the others. Do not make the mistake of thinking no one will notice differences in these areas of connection with your kids. They will notice, and the message you will be sending is: "You are not valued as the others."

Two of our sons live in the same urban area, which is some 1,500 miles from where my wife and I live. When visiting, we are aware that both families want to spend time with Grandma and Grandpa. What I was surprised to learn is that all the grandchildren are counting the days the grandparents spend at each household as if they were keeping score. None of them want to be shorted!

Adults who are serious about avoiding the sin of partiality will also recognize that we are all responsible for modeling God's love to those within our sphere of influence (James 2:9). We must take this issue seriously and be obedient to Scripture as we interact with others.

Making Amends for Favoritism

Many adults, young and old, feel they have been treated unjustly by family members in the past. In such cases, the best recourse is to have a heart-to-heart discussion with all involved, approaching this interaction in all humility. Without discussion, this resentment will not go away but will continue to fester. If you find yourself a part of such a discussion, remember that listening is typically more than half of the interaction you need to have. Do not go into this endeavor with a predetermined outcome in mind. You may learn things that clarify why past decisions were made. If you are the adult who has shown preferential treatment in the past, you can also use this approach to "clear the air" and even ask for forgiveness, if that is warranted.

Since partiality can ruin the picture of God's undeserved love for us, we all must be willing to address this potential area of sin, especially with those we love. In our earlier example, Sam should have this discussion with his parents, rather than hoping everything will turn out favorably for him when the family estate is being settled at some future date. Without some action or explanation by Fred and Linda, there will certainly be some hard feelings between the surviving siblings in the future. Christians are called to do better in our relationships!

Chapter 12
Technology

Not long ago, staying in touch with loved ones meant long-distance phone calls and per-minute phone charges, handwritten letters, and waiting weeks for a photo to arrive by mail. Today, with just a few taps on a screen, you can see your grandchild's smile in real time, share a quick text with your adult children, or even join a birthday party via video call. Technology has transformed the way we stay connected. But with that convenience comes new challenges we must navigate thoughtfully and graciously.

Technology is not optional in today's society. It is happening all around us and affects nearly every aspect of our lives, regardless of how engaged we are in the details of our technological world. Technology can be a tremendous blessing in our lives when used wisely, or it can be a curse if we allow it to become a consuming passion or misuse it.[1]

Using Technology Wisely

When used wisely, technology can make our lives easier and less stressful. It is no longer necessary to remember to write that monthly payment check on schedule. Automatic scheduled payments or other electronic op-

---

1 Peter Goeman, *Artificial Intelligence and the Christian: Understanding AI's Promises and Pitfalls* (Raleigh, NC: Sojourner Press, 2024), 48.

tions can be more convenient, more stress-free, and safer when used correctly. Yet, despite all the benefits, it is important for everyone to realize that technology brings with it inherent risks. Personal information falling into the hands of an unscrupulous individual could become very costly. This reality should not paralyze us with fear, but we must be aware of the potential dangers and take appropriate steps to ensure that we do not become the next victims.

If you or someone you love is uncomfortable using technology, they should have the option of using more traditional, non-technological means of conducting their personal affairs, assuming those options are available. If a person is willing to use technology, but needs to learn how, we should be willing to patiently help them become proficient enough to move into the technological realm in a safe manner.

Managing Expectations in a Technological World

Some people take great joy in posting every event of their lives on social media for their friends and the rest of the world to see. Others take a more guarded view of what, if anything, personal gets posted. Neither approach is right or wrong. Technological preferences should never be allowed to negatively influence our relationships. Good communication is key in considering another person's preferences ahead of your own desires.

This is especially true in the realm of grandparents and the families of their adult children. In managing our expectations and those of others in the world of technology, it may be helpful to revisit biblical authority. Recall that biblical authority refers to that which God has specifically authorized in His Word.[2] For example, parents have authority over their dependent (young) children. Grandparents do not have parental authority over their grandchildren; neither do parents have authority over their adult children. It is also helpful to distinguish between areas of concern and areas of responsibility. I may have concerns regarding my adult children posting pictures of my grandchildren on social media, but I am not responsible for such actions regarding my grandchildren.

"Good communication is key in considering another person's preferences ahead of your own desires."

Practical Tips and Advice

The world of technology and cybersecurity is changing so rapidly that it is impossible to provide guidance that will be current regarding specifics. However, the list that follows will provide sufficient detail to help us think biblically about this topic.

1. Grant deference to others in matters of preference. Deference involves thinking the best about others and assuming they have the right motivation.

2. Communicate with others about technology, particularly if this clarifies how you interact with another who has biblical authority. Grandparents, this means you will abide by the wishes

---

2 See the discussion on "Biblical Authority" (Chapter 2), 11-16.

of the parents when it comes to decisions like posting or not posting pictures of your beloved grandchildren on social media, or how much screen time a grandchild is allowed.

3. Endeavor to understand the reason for another's preferences. In some cases, there are legitimate safety concerns surrounding social media activity. Again, in thinking through this topic, simply consider another person's desires as more important than your own, and most conflicts can be avoided.

4. If another person is uncomfortable with any aspect of technology, they should never be forced to operate in this realm. If it is a matter of training or learning, be patient as the teacher.

5. If technology-based communication becomes too frequent or not frequent enough, discuss this with your loved one.

6. Understand that some issues must be discussed in person, and technological options are not appropriate. Major life decisions or events fall into this category.

7. Remember that your use of technology should serve as a model for children or grandchildren. Seek to please the Lord in all things. Never communicate anything via social media that you would not say to another in person.

8. Know when to stow your devices. Many in the older generation consider it rude to use a mobile phone or tablet during a meal together.

9. In-person visits are highly prized by many in our culture, and families should cherish these times. During an in-person visit, make every effort to put the cell phone away. Many older adults consider it very rude to have a guest more consumed with their phone than they are with the person in their presence. If this presents too great a challenge for you, leave your phone in your car or at home. As amazing as it sounds, there was a time when no one carried a cell phone everywhere they went, and they all survived! Many will argue that they cannot abide by this advice for a number of reasons, but again, consider others as more important than yourself (Phil. 2:3-4).

10. If you see an area of a relationship where technology could make an improvement, ask the other person if this will work for them. If they are a little unsure, but are willing to try, help them set things up to demonstrate the advantages. Our church recently offered financial assistance to one of our members to help with a crisis in their life. I was tasked with getting them the funds. I asked, via text message, if they preferred cash or used a P2P (peer-to-peer) payment system. It turns out they were able to receive the money with the push of a button on my cell phone. How convenient for everyone! But again, such a solution is only appropriate if everyone is comfortable with it, and you will only know that by asking.

Technology is a reality in our society, but we must collectively strive to make it our servant, rather than becoming enslaved to it. Consider others, communicate well, and grant deference to them; technology can be a great enhancement to our lives.

Chapter 13

Bringing it All Together

This short book has been about ensuring that your actions as a Christian parent of an adult child match up with what the Scriptures teach about how to live in relationship with others. In my experience, parents entering this final stage of parenting have largely been left to themselves with little guidance. As a result, most people are left to work through this stage of life on their own. From a distance, this may seem simple enough. After all, we are talking about parents who have been through years of child training and have presumably been growing in their own sanctification. However, reality has shown that sometimes our theology has been lacking, and our sanctification has not progressed as it should have. Add in the emotions as we cope with all the changes facing our late teen and early 20s kids, and too often, we may respond to them inappropriately.

As you have read the preceding pages, perhaps you have found yourself bristling at some of the ideas and concepts. These biblical principles will only make sense to Christians who understand the authority of the Bible in their lives. Additionally, we all need to be reminded that our own, well-intentioned, humanly derived approaches to relationships will always be poor substitutes for God's ways.

Secular philosophies can exert more influence on us than we might think if we are not grounded in Scripture. Ideas like allowing young adults more time to pre-

pare for independence, providing shelter for those not
able to deal with

"In God's providence, every child is born to become a functional, independent adult."

the anxieties of life, or concerns about a young adult's emotional health are all secular attempts to address spiritual problems. In life, there is God's way as defined in the Bible, and there is the human counterfeit that might sound good but can never address the real problem. Christian parents must never be content to sacrifice God's way, which may be more difficult, for anything less. In God's providence, every child is born to become a functional, independent adult.

If a theme verse is helpful in adopting the right thinking about this final stage of parenting, it would be Romans 12:3: "For through the grace given to me I say to each one among you not to think more highly of himself than he ought to think; but to think so as to have sound thinking, as God has allotted to each a measure of faith." Your children have grown into actual people, independent adults. You must not hinder that reality.

Summarizing Key Concepts

As discussed earlier, you can still contribute to their lives, but now it is an adult-to-adult relationship, and it is only when you are invited. Too many parents fail to grasp this reality, and the result is one adult trying to force, coerce, cajole, or manipulate another adult into doing something or being someone they resist. Don't be those parents! The lives of your adult children are not about you. If you are more concerned about your reputation, family traditions, or some other aspect of what you think life should be, regardless of what your young adult wants, you may be an idolater. Recall that an idol is anything or anyone that captures our hearts, minds, and affections more than God. When we desire something so intensely that we are willing to sin to obtain it, we have an idol in our lives.

Obedience and honor are foundational topics addressed in great detail in Scripture, but are poorly understood and practiced by many Christians. Our culture has tainted the biblical truths regarding these essential subjects to the detriment of our relationships and even our society. Regardless of your age, you will benefit yourself and those you love by practicing what Scripture teaches—and start now.

Our speech reveals a lot about what is really in our hearts (Luke 6:45). If you catch yourself saying things to your loved ones that should never be said, it is time for some heart evaluation. Or, if a friend or spouse challenges you regarding your speech, do not react negatively in the flesh, but consider whether this is the appropriate way for an ambassador of Christ to be speaking.

The wedding of your child should be a joyous occasion for everyone. As parents of the bride or groom, back off and let them take charge of their special day. Help where you can when you are asked, but recognize that you are in the background of this event. You had your day when you got married—this is not your day as the parent.

If a situation arises where your children return home as adults, don't panic. Although this was probably never in your plan, handle this situation wisely, lovingly, but firmly, and it can become a positive piece of past history before long. Life is full of difficulties, and this does not mean the end of life as you know it. Remember that you have complete control over your home and what happens within its walls. Adulthood carries with it many privileges, but also commensurate responsibilities. These two aspects of life are inseparable. You simply cannot have one without the other. If your adult children have not grasped this important, non-negotiable concept, you must lovingly but firmly help them get there. Adolescence was never meant to last for decades!

A goal that all parents should strive for is to become good friends with their adult children. This ideal is not beyond your grasp. To make it a reality, you must adopt a new mode in relating to your kids. Treat them as adults. Respect their opinions and decisions, don't force your ideas on anyone. Keep unwarranted criticism out of your vocabulary. Provide assistance and advice when asked, as you are able. Love them for who they are.

When you visit the home of your adult children, remember that you are a guest and not a visiting monarch. Do all you can to make your visit a positive experience for your hosts. Take on the attitude of a servant for your entire stay. After all, in doing so you will be modeling your Lord!

Regarding grandchildren, remember two truths: (1) they are not your children, and (2) they are your grandchildren. I encourage every grandparent to search the Scriptures to understand the differing functions of parents and grandparents. Don't miss out on the joys of being grandparents. "Grandchildren are the crown of the aged" (Prov. 17:6a).

For your children and grandchildren, avoid the sin of partiality. Favoritism cannot be masked. Everyone knows when it happens, and it can destroy relationships for a lifetime. Do not be deceived—this is sin, even though we might like to place it in the category of "respectable sins."

Finally, only use technology to enhance relationships in your life. Recognize that what you consider normal, others may find offensive. Always be diligent to recognize matters of preference for what they are, considering others before yourself.

Important End of Life Considerations

This book has been about how parents can interact with their adult children in a biblical, Christ-exalting manner. Although there could be much more said on almost every issue, I have tried to be brief in my discussion. Yet, we could not conclude a book about the relationship between parents and their adult children without a few comments on end of life matters. So, here are four actions all parents should take as acts of love for their children:

1. Buy a cemetery plot and headstone for yourself and your spouse. If you prefer a different option, make that known and make those arrangements. Your children will thank you for taking care of

this detail rather than putting this burden upon them during their time of grief.

2. Complete a healthcare directive that expresses your wishes for your health care if you are unable to communicate your wishes at some future time.

3. Appoint a power-of-attorney to handle your life affairs if you are unable to do so.

4. Complete a will or a trust to ensure that your estate is administered appropriately and efficiently after your death.

Yes, I know. Do we really need to think about these things? Yes, please take care of these details for those you will leave behind someday, if the Lord doesn't return first. You are taking these actions out of love for others. These steps are a matter of good stewardship on your part—right up to the end of life.

The Bridge Builder

By Will Allen Dromgoole[1]

An old man going a lone highway,
Came, at the evening cold and gray,
To a chasm vast and deep and wide.
Through which was flowing a sullen tide
The old man crossed in the twilight dim,
The sullen stream had no fear for him;
But he turned when safe on the other side
And built a bridge to span the tide.

"Old man," said a fellow pilgrim near,
"You are wasting your strength with building here;
Your journey will end with the ending day,
You never again will pass this way;
You've crossed the chasm, deep and wide,
Why build this bridge at evening tide?"

The builder lifted his old gray head;
"Good friend, in the path I have come," he said,
"There followed after me to-day

---

1 The poem can be found at https://www.poetryfoundation.org/
poems/52702/the-bridge-builder.

A youth whose feet must pass this way.
This chasm that has been as naught to me
To that fair-haired youth may a pitfall be;
He, too, must cross in the twilight dim;
Good friend, I am building this bridge for him!"

Questions & Answers

1. My adult child (age 30, living on their own) continues to make bad decisions and some are even immoral. How can I "fix" them?

A: You cannot "fix" another person. Because change begins in the heart, you can only change yourself. That being said, Paul encouraged Timothy to reprove, rebuke, and exhort, with complete patience and teaching (2 Tim. 4:2). Although you have no direct authority over the life of your adult child, you can warn them of the consequences of deliberately continuing in sin. As painful as it may be, consider the possibility that they may not be saved. If they are an unbeliever, they do not have the capacity to think rightly or act rightly. That being said, you should never participate in or support their immoral lifestyle choices. Finally, make sure that your issues with this young adult are not matters of preference.

2. I realize I have made some big mistakes in raising my children and even in how I have treated them disrespectfully as adults. What do I do now?

A: Confess these sins to your children and ask their forgiveness, in all humility. If your repentance is real, all is not lost. Forgiveness is a powerful act that can produce indescribably wonderful results (1 John 1:8-9).

3. I have a very difficult relationship with my aging parents. We have never been close and have never gotten along very well. You could even say we are estranged. How can I possibly honor them at this point in life?

A: In all humility, commit your circumstances to prayer, asking God to show you the next steps. This might be as simple as a visit for a few hours. It is possible that your act of reaching out may be rejected, and if that's the case, you may have done all you can do. But maybe this could be the start of a more meaningful relationship. The reality is that you will never know unless you take the first steps, in humility.

4. I have the classic case of a young adult living in my home. He does not work, has no plans for the future, and just won't leave. What can I do?

A: If your spouse is in the picture, discuss the situation with them first and agree on a plan. The last thing you need is your young adult pitting you, as parents, against each other. Have a discussion with your young adult about what needs to change, setting mutually agreed upon goals, and a timeline for when these goals might be accomplished. Put them in writing. If your young adult refuses to discuss things, you can evict them. This is your house, and in some cases, this may be the most loving thing you can do.

5. As a newly married young couple, my spouse continues to go to his/her mother for advice and counsel, generally leaving me out of the picture altogether. What should I do?

A: Have a discussion with your spouse about the husband-wife relationship being the priority, with all other human relationships being secondary to it. If this does not go well, you may need to involve your pastor or a trusted Christian counselor. The priority of marriage is God's way and God's design, and when followed, is a beautiful thing. Man's way—in this case, involving the mother ahead of the spouse—will always fall short.

6. I see other parents and their adult kids who seem to have great relationships, but that is not how things are with my adult children. I can't put my finger on any specific problem, but it just seems like it could be better.

A: Avoid the trap of comparing your life with that of others around you. Discontentment is sure to result. Relationships take time and require nurturing. If you are not aware of specific sins that you should deal with, ask your adult children if you are missing something. Then, take some deliberate steps to nurture these relationships in a positive direction. However, realize that all relationships involve two sinful people, and because people are inherently different, each relationship will take on its own unique character.

7. My adult child is living in my home, and I have tried to discuss setting goals toward becoming functional and independent. Still, they won't even discuss the topic. Whenever I try to have this discussion with them, they walk out of the room. As a parent, I really feel stuck.

A: You are not stuck, but you do need to set your emotions aside and show your adult child some "tough love." He should be evicted from your home. To allow this behavior to continue is neither loving nor wise. You should prepare yourself that your young adult will tell you that you are unloving, uncaring, and he has a right to live in this house, but this is simply manipulative behavior. Your adult child's desire is to continue in an irresponsible lifestyle. Your desire is that they grow up, become functional and independent. Until something changes, neither of these desires nor their accompanying behaviors will change. You can only change your part of the equation, since your child refuses to discuss this. Truly, your only recourse is eviction.

8. We have one of our adult children who has moved back home. He has no job, no money, no discipline, and no desire to do anything but eat and watch TV. I want to follow some of the steps outlined in this book to move them toward functionality and independence, but my spouse is afraid that if we take any action it will hurt our adult child emotionally, and he will think we don't love him. What can I do?

A: You and your spouse need to be convinced of the right actions by Scripture, not by crafty human argument. If you are unable to accomplish this as a couple, seek help from your pastor or a trusted Christian counselor. We can only have absolute confidence in our actions if we are convinced by the authority of Scripture.

9. We came to an agreement with our adult child who is living in our home, and we even put it in writing. But after a few months, several major parts of our agreement are being violated regularly—such things as not paying the agreed-upon rent, use of alcohol, etc. Now what do we do?

A: You have a contract that has been broken. The worst possible response from you is to do nothing. Doing nothing reinforces the undesirable behavior. Appropriate consequences are warranted, including possible eviction. Do your best to make sure the "punishment fits the crime."

10. Our adult child has grown up, sort of. He lives on his own and is pretty much independent, except when it comes to money. He routinely asks us for money (at least twice a month). I know he has a good-paying job, but I also know there is a good deal of irresponsible spending going on. Help!

A: If you want something to change, you cannot keep doing the same thing. In this case, giving your child money whenever he asks for it. This young adult needs some financial help setting up a budget and then living by it. You should suggest this, and of course, your leverage is to cut off the financial handouts. This is a case where you can offer counsel, but should also refuse to participate in irresponsible financial behavior by your young adult.

11. Our 18-year-old has a few months of high school left before graduation, but has broken our trust (and our hearts) by hosting a party at our house when we went out of town for the weekend. There were many illegal things that happened at the party. What should we do?

A: Much of your response will be dictated by your young adult's attitude toward his sin. If he is truly repentant and is willing to adopt a plan of repentance, this may be a positive step in his spiritual development, from a long-term perspective. Even in the best-case scenario, parents should draw up some written requirements for him to continue living in their house and have him sign it. This step will ensure he grasps the gravity of his sin. If his attitude is one of defiance because he is now an adult, requiring him to leave the house may be the best recourse for everyone.

12. My wife and I have three children under 6 years old, and we have observed the increasing number of dysfunctional young adults in our society. What can we do to ensure our kids don't end up like that?

A: In addition to the spiritual input and guidance that is essential, here are some simple, practical, but seemingly forgotten practices that can help put your kids on the right trajectory to adulthood: teach them about the blessings and discipline of work, don't allow laziness or excuses to be a part of who they are, teach them about the benefit of schedules and financial stewardship. Your local church should be a place where all of these life principles are practiced and reinforced. Of primary importance, as parents, model these scriptural truths as examples for your kids to follow.

13. Our son is more or less independent, but his former bedroom in our home is pretty much as he left it, complete with his computer. Periodically, he will show up, sequester himself in his old room overnight or for a day or two, and then leave. He has little interaction with us, and we feel we're being used. Is this okay? What should we do.

A: This is your home, and you can use it as you see fit (or prevent someone else from using it if you don't approve). It might be wise to "repurpose" his old bedroom into a bona fide guest room or study. Freshen it up. Move his computer out. Have a discussion with him about giving you some prior notice if he wants to spend the night (with your approval). Have him take his computer out of your house. If you are willing to make some reasonable changes, you can help move him toward more acceptable behavior in your home.

14. My husband and I have done a pretty fair job of training our four kids. They all love the Lord and are active in our church as young adults. We also do our best to treat them as adults. Our only problem is that we occasionally slip back into "control mode," where we offer unsolicited advice or even try to intervene directly in their lives to produce a better outcome, without being asked. We know it's wrong, but how can we stop?

A: You are in the commendable position of recognizing that your actions are wrong. Let's push this out into the light a little more and recognize it as sin! Remember that all sin is first and foremost against God. This reality should give all of us pause when we think about these types of behaviors. Practically, I have also found it is helpful to verbalize the truth that "they're adults now." Sometimes stating this factual statement to your spouse or friends who are in a similar stage of life can help us reset our thinking quickly.

15. The information in this book has been interesting, but I don't think it deals with reality. My life is different and way more complex than has been discussed here. As a result, I am not convinced that any of this applies to me.

A: It is very common for all of us to think that we are the exception. Just remember the words of Jeremiah 17:9 regarding our deceitful hearts. The thing about being deceived is that you don't know it's happening. This is why we need the local church and the cleansing power of the Word in our lives regularly. Most of us think we are doing better than we are. For God's glory, all Christians should ensure that we are striving for relationships that are all God intended them to be.

16. My child has a medically diagnosed mental condition that genuinely affects the goals of parenting you propose. How should we adapt as parents?

A: Every situation involving these challenges will be unique, but parents should still accomplish all that God allows in terms of the goals of parenting. I know of several special-needs children who have a saving knowledge of God due, in part, to the diligent work of the parents. Parents should also teach their special children about a biblical worldview to the fullest extent of their child's comprehension. The goals of functionality and independence will certainly be uniquely constrained and dictated by each child's capability. Nonetheless, we must never underestimate God's grace as faithful parents train up these children for God's glory.

17. Our believing son just informed us he is about to be engaged to an unbeliever. How should we respond?

A: Such a decision by a young man indicates that he is either very immature in the faith or not a Christian at all. Such thinking ignores many important doctrinal truths, including: the preeminence of Christ in the life of the believer, the inability of unbelievers to understand spiritual things, and the eternal destiny of the unbeliever. All of these and more should be lovingly discussed with your son by you and your pastor or a trusted Christian counselor. You should also recognize that your son is an adult, so your authority in his life is limited to counsel. He can choose to marry whoever he wants, as painful as that may be.

18. Our adult son's actions have confirmed for my wife and me that it is time for him to move out of our home after almost 3 years. How can we have this conversation?

A: Prayerfully develop a plan for precisely what needs to be discussed based on the particulars of your situation. You should affirm your love for him, but stick to your decision. You can expect push-back in terms of manipulative behavior or comments from him. If he refuses to have a conversation or walks out during your meeting, post your equivalent of an eviction notice on the door of his room. Be very clear about when he needs to go. Do not feel compelled to help him find alternative housing. As an adult, that is his responsibility. In some extreme cases, parents have had to physically remove the adult child's belongings and have the locks on the doors changed! Remember that this is love in action.

19. My spouse and I have taken the difficult step of evicting our adult son from our home after intense discussions about our expectations, but his moral failures and ungodly attitudes continued. We are confident we did the right thing. The issue is that his grandparents have now taken him in and are giving him free rein, allowing him to do whatever he wants, and are supporting him financially. What should we do?

A: You can explain to the grandparents why you did what you did and the history of your son's past behavior, but you have no authority over their household. You might show them the example of Eli and his sons, and explain that God must be honored before our children and grandchildren. Continue to pray for your son and his grandparents, but as painful as this is for you, you have no control over the decisions of others.

20. Our daughter just went through a nasty divorce and has now been left to raise her two young children alone. They have moved into our home. As grandparents, how can we help her?

A: There is no one-size-fits-all answer to this difficult question. Certainly your role as grandparents will have components that may not be relevant to other families who are not in these circumstances. Nonetheless, many of the basics discussed in this book will still apply. For instance, your daughter should still move toward independence, even if this involves a "10-year plan." She is still the responsible parent, and you are grandparents, playing "supporting roles." As a grandfather, you will never be a father to your grandchildren, but you can be a godly, male role model. By God's grace, your daughter's family can not only survive, but they can thrive. Maintain open communication with your daughter about her thoughts and needs. Search the Scriptures for guidance as issues arise, and then prayerfully ask for the wisdom to apply it. Trust in the sovereignty of our loving heavenly Father.

21. As a parent of young adults, should my daughter be treated differently than my son regarding the goals of being independent and functional? Some Christian fathers claim their adult daughter should stay in their home under their headship until she is married (sometimes known as the "daughters-at-home" movement).

A: While I assume this approach to "protecting" our daughters arises from genuine love and concern, I do not believe it is a scriptural mandate that daughters must remain at home until marriage. Our young adult daughters will be best served by becoming independent and functional just like their brothers, although the exact process and timing may vary. The ancient cultures of Bible times often treated young women differently than we do today in the Western world. We should not make the error of selecting one aspect of biblical culture and superimposing it on how we live today. Furthermore, we can't be sure that God has not called our young, adult daughter to a life of singleness. Although the Bible prioritizes the role of wife and mother, we must concede that God may choose to use women in other ways, and they must be prepared for those potential realities. Becoming independent and functional in today's culture is the best preparation for all that God has for your daughter in adulthood—whether that includes marriage or singleness.

Epilogue

Most people will at least consider counsel that is offered, if it seems reasonable. If this advice is also supported by Scripture, it carries additional weight, particularly for Christians. When Bible-based advice is further substantiated by positive effects in the lives of real people, we all tend to listen closer, believe more deeply and apply with more determined conviction.

To that end, I have asked my three adult sons and their wives (ages 35–41) to express a few thoughts about this book. I want to be clear before going any further that my wife and I did not parent perfectly, and we do not even claim to relate to our adult kids perfectly, but we are fully convinced of the right direction, and for that we are striving daily. It is only our flesh that prevents us from being better parents, grandparents and friends to these wonderful young adults God has put in our lives.

I asked our young adults, "How are we doing as your parents now that you are adults? Are we offering the right balance of encouragement and support without being controlling or critical of your decisions? Have we been there when you needed us, but given you all the freedom you wanted as adults? Do you consider us to be your friends?"

Here are some of their responses.

Testimony of Daughter-in-Law

You are great parents. You allow us to be grown-ups and make adult decisions without being controlling. At the same time you balance that with a genuine interest in what is going on in our lives, which makes us feel loved. The conversations are easy and it's fun to share with you. You also make it easy to come to you for advice, even if the topics are difficult. We know you will not judge us and you give us sound advice. We do consider you as friends. We genuinely enjoy your company, we can laugh with you, we can cry with you—it's a relationship that we treasure.

Testimony of Son

You always seem to be willing to be involved in our lives whenever we ask. When we talk I come away feeling encouraged and supported. I cannot recall a time when you, as parents, have tried to control us or our decisions. You have always been willing to give feedback or your thoughts, but only when we have asked for it. Best of all, you have always been there when we needed you, but you have never impinged on our freedom as adults or our own family's independent functioning. Bottom line—as parents you are great friends, always there, day or night. Even when I am not as good of a friend as I should be, that does not diminish the friendship that exists. Whenever we look to you, there you are, arms wide open.

Testimony of Son

As parents, you have never meddled in our day-to-day lives. We can get your opinions and advice on being good parents and spouses, but only when we ask. However, you are always encouraging us to grow in the faith. You have typically made yourselves available and are godly examples of humble servants. We thoroughly enjoy your company and friendship. I view you as some of my best friends. We proactively seek to spend time with each other. You are a part of our kids' lives, but the grandkids are never prioritized above our relationship, which I appreciate. An aspect of the friendship that has really hit me in recent days is that not only do we seek your guidance and input on various aspects of our lives, but you now seek input and guidance from us in certain areas of your lives.

Testimony of Son

I am so thankful to the Lord for you as our parents. My wife and I feel immensely privileged to have a deep and lasting friendship with you. While it is true that Christ has given older and wiser men and women to the church to help younger families learn, it is a privilege when we can find that valuable relationship with our own parents. We love how you are always serving and never presuming upon us to meet your needs. We always feel served and refreshed by your visits, and we regularly feel motivated to follow your example in the way you love and care for us as a family. We cherish the mature and Christ-honoring conversations we have with you. As adult children, we truly feel that we benefit from having friends who inspire us to love the Lord and serve Him more faithfully. Thank you!

Testimony of Daughter-in-Law

When I married my husband I knew I was getting the cream of the crop, but what I didn't know at the time was that I had hit the in-law jackpot! Tim and Julie have been such a blessing to me and my family. I treasure their friendship, counsel, and words of encouragement. They have supported us at every turn, have been boots on the ground during some of the most challenging seasons of life, have selflessly served us in more ways than can be listed, and pray for us continually. Their example of faithfulness encourages me to live likewise and to follow them as they follow Christ.